THE NEW CREATION!

THE 'BORN AGAIN' PHENOMENA

FELIPE A. GUZMAN

TABLE OF CONTENT

All scripture in this book is taken from the New King James Version unless otherwise noted. All emphasis on scripture is given by this author.

Jesus came only for the "lost sheep of the house of Israel," Matthew 15:24, but sent the Holy Spirit as a 'free gift' to the entire world upon His ascension. Why? Because the Jews were the only people on earth who the Messiah belonged to and should have recognized who He was. The rest of the world had no spiritual or religious connection, knowledge or inclination to know anything about a Jewish Messiah. The Jews were not only God's chosen people they were His created nation and race. He made Himself know to them and had an intimate relationship with them. After their rejection of their Messiah and according to His perfect plan, He turned to the Gentiles. Born-again believers, whether Jew or Gentile, are the 'New Creation,' and therefore, the true Israel, spoken of in the New Testament scriptures.

INTRODUCTION

This book is about the realities of the physical and immaterial composition of all human beings, and most importantly, the one who is now 'born-again.' The main source of reference for this book comes from the Holy Bible, for it is only in the Holy Scriptures that we can gain a true understanding of what it means to be 'born-again' into a *new creation* as expressed to us, by God Himself, in His word. When reading the Bible, context is extremely important. Understanding words, phrases, and complete thoughts of the author in their proper context is essential for the truth of God's word to set us free from the bondage of the world, Satan and our own minds. Take for instance the word, 'world.' This word in scripture takes on different meanings and will only make meaningful sense when context is taken into consideration. The word 'world,' can mean; this physical universe, a past, present or future age, a reference to a specific time in history, certain types of people such as nonbelievers, or it can even mean a specific ideology.

In like manner understanding the words; *flesh, soul* and *spirit* in context of its intended meaning will make the difference between, rightly dividing the word of truth and making false conclusion that lead to false beliefs, which upon application of those false beliefs can lead us into much confusion and can even lead some to fall away from the faith. The word 'flesh,' like the word 'world,' has multiple meanings in the Bible. It can be used in a literal sense, such as in, *"All flesh is not the same flesh, but there is one kind of flesh of men, another flesh of animals, another of fish, and another of birds,"* 1 Corinthians 15:39. The word 'flesh' can also be used in a general sense such as in referring to a total person when differentiating between a non-believer and a true born-again believer in Christ. *"Those who are in the flesh cannot please God," Romans 8:8.* 'Those who are in the flesh,' does not mean that every person walking around in a human body is displeasing to God, rather, 'in the flesh,' in this passage of scripture is referring to a person of the world, in love with the world, a person who is not saved, not regenerated and does not have the Holy Spirit living in him or her, or in other words, as Jesus stated, not *'born-again'* (John 3:3). It is a person who obviously has no belief, much less faith, in God and, therefore, it is impossible for that person, 'in the flesh' to please God.

The words 'flesh' and 'body' appear to be synonymous, for example the word 'flesh,' can mean; the actual 'body' of Christ as in Jesus' physical, body. The word 'soul,' means the immaterial part of our 'self,' that holds our; consciousness, mind, heart, reasoning, desires, etc...., that we use to express our thoughts and feelings. The word 'soul' can also be used in a general emotional sense such as when expressing one's feelings. *"Mary said, my **soul** does magnify the Lord, and my spirit has rejoiced in God my Savior," Luke 1:46.* Notice how Mary expresses a distinction between her soul and her spirit. The following passage of scripture; *"And fear came upon every **soul**," Acts 2:43,* is using the word 'soul' as referring to a group of people, as a whole; people with a body, soul and spirit and not disembodied souls floating around with no physical body or spirit.

We now come to the word 'spirit.' There is much confusion about what people believe is the *spirit*. I do not contend that I can fully explain that which many scholars seem to disagree on when it comes to explaining the 'spirit.' The soul and spirit are clearly depicted as distinct entities numerous times in the Bible and since God is not a God of confusion, He must have a reason for declaring to us that we are; soul and spirit in a body, *"Now may the God of peace Himself sanctify you completely; and may your whole **spirit, soul,** and **body** be found blameless at the coming of our Lord Jesus Christ,"* 1 Thessalonians 5:23.

The soul and spirit, although both being nonphysical, can be, as declared in God's word, separated or divided from each other, and as we will soon learn, it is imperative that they be separated, *"For the word of God is living and powerful, and sharper than any two-edged sword, piercing even to the **<u>division</u> of soul and spirit**,"* Hebrews 4:12. There is also a distinction between the body and the spirit in the book of John; *"That which is born of flesh is flesh and that which is born of Spirit is spirit,"* John 3:6 . So, we have here scriptures that give us a clear description of the human composition; body, soul and spirit, each can, needs to and will be separated from one another as we journey through this life. How do these three aspects of our human composition work together, yet separately? When we are conceived in our mother's womb, we are conceived with a spirit and a soul in physical matter that soon becomes a complete person, that is in constant change. In our basic form our spirit is what makes us exist, or be alive, while our physical body is what is needed to manipulate and move around in, in this physical world, with our soul being the immaterial vehicle that allows us to experience mentally, emotionally and physically this world we are born into.

Every person born into this world is born with a body, a soul and a spirit completely 'dead' to God and extremely alive to this 'world system.' Every person born into this world is in desperate need of being regenerated or in other words in need of salvation, starting with being born-again, if one wishes to spend eternity with God in heaven; *"Most assuredly I say to you,* **unless one is born-again,** *he cannot see the kingdom of God," John 3:3.* As we will learn, it is the spirit that is regenerated, made perfect, sanctified and holy at the time he or she receives Jesus as Lord and Savior and becomes 'born-again.'

Upon receiving Christ Jesus, our spirit is 'spiritually' set apart from our body and soul, and from the power of this deluded world system, as well as the demonic control or influences. It is a spiritual separation and a transformation of our spirit, that has been made perfect and holy by God Himself, through the infilling of the Holy Spirit. The 'born-again' spirit of the believer is now set apart from the body and soul. This separation and transformation are spiritual and not visible or noticeable to the physical senses as scripture clearly states; *"That which is born of the flesh is flesh, and that which is born of the Spirit is spirit. Do not marvel that I said to you, 'You must be born again.' The wind blows where it wishes, and you hear the sound of it, but cannot tell where it comes from and where it goes. So is everyone who is born of the Spirit, John 3:6-8.* *"In Him you were circumcised with the* **circumcision made without hands,** *by putting off the body of the sins of the flesh, by the* **circumcision of Christ,** **buried with Him** *in baptism, in which you also were* **raised with Him** through faith in the working of God, who raised Him from the dead, Colossians 2:11-13.*

*"**They are not of the world**, just as I am not of the world...I do not pray for these alone but also for those who will believe in Me through their word; that they all may be one, as You, Father, are in Me, and I in You, that **they also may be one in Us**,"* John 17:16, 20,21. *"But God who is rich in mercy, because of His great love with which He loves us, even when we were dead in our trespasses, **made us alive** together with Christ (by grace you have been saved), and raised us up together and **made us sit together in the heavenly places** in Christ Jesus,"* Ephesians 2:4-6. *"If then you were raised with Christ, seek those things which are above, where Christ is sitting at the right hand of God. Set your mind on things above, not on things on earth. For **you died, and your life is hidden with Christ in God,**_"*Colossians 3:1-3.

The above scriptures clearly indicate that every born-again believer; 1.) Is not of this world, 2.) Is in Christ Jesus and God the Father, .3) Was once dead, but is now alive to God, 4.) Has been raised with Christ, from the dead, 5.) Is sitting with Christ, right now, in heavenly places, and 6.) Their life is now hidden, not visible, unseen, with Christ *IN GOD!* This may sound counter-intuitive, due to the fact, that if you are reading this right now, you are here on earth. You know that you are either standing, sitting, or laying down somewhere reading this book, so how could you be 'sitting in heavenly places' right now? How is it that you can see your life lived out here on earth and yet at the same time, your life be hidden in Christ who is sitting at the right hand of God the Father?

Not many people stop to contemplate the reality of their own existence much less their total composition as a person; body, soul and spirit. By the time you finish reading this book you should have a good understanding of the reality of your composition as a human being here on earth and the real self, hidden in Christ, as a born-again new-creation. Our spirit is the place that God's Holy Spirit resides and where a person receives the things communicated by God through the Holy Spirit living in their spirit, which in turn, is received by our consciousness/mind (soul), to which the believer, using his/her freewill (soul), acts on through the workings of the body that works out what God is asking the believer to do or say, *"For we are His workmanship created in Christ Jesus for good works, which God prepared beforehand, that we should walk in them,"* *Ephesians 2:6.*

Although we perceive ourselves as one entity, the reality is that we are three different entities; body, soul and spirit with each entity having a different function and depending of what a person decides to do upon hearing the gospel of Jesus Christ, where their soul and spirit will spend eternity. God is the Father, the Son and the Holy Spirit, three persons in one essence, not three Gods in one God, nor three Essences in one Essence nor three Persons in one Person, but rather three Persons in one God; the Father, the Son and the Holy Spirit! God, according to scripture, consists of three distinct persons that make up the God-head or the Trinity.

This Trinity is a mystery that only upon entrance into the heavenly realm, at the end of our earthly life, and as we step into the ultimate spiritual reality, will we truly know Him as He is; God the Father, Jesus the Son and the Holy Spirit-The Holy Trinity.

Jesus clearly stated that He and the Father were one, *"My sheep hear My voice and I know them, and they follow Me. And I give them eternal life, and they shall never perish; neither shall anyone snatch them out of My hand. My Father, who has given them to Me, is greater than all; and no one is able to snatch them out of My Father's hand.* **I and My Father are one**,*"* John 10:27-29.

Jesus also alluded to the reality of the trinity as well as the fact that He Himself was the Holy Spirit, *"If you love* **Me***, keep my commandments, "And I will pray the* **Father,** *and He will give you another* **Helper***, that He may abide with you forever, "the Spirit of Truth, whom the world cannot receive, because it neither sees Him nor knows Him,* **but you know Him, for He dwells with you** *and will be* **in you.** *I will not leave you orphans; I will come to you,"* John 14:15-18.

The above scripture implicitly speaks of a triune God; the Father, the Son and the Holy Spirit. However, not only do these scriptures allude to the trinity, they also imply that the disciples already know **who** the Holy Spirit, whom the world neither sees or knows, is, because, He (the Holy Spirit), is dwells with them (Jesus was dwelling with them!). There are many scriptures that reveal that God is a Triune God; the Father, the Son and the Holy Spirit. One only need study and search the scriptures with an open mind and heart to see the reality of our Triune God that we serve. Since both spirit and soul are immaterial aspects of what we are, and since God Himself is Spirit, it should be easy to understand how the immaterial part of who and what we are, is analogous to God in that the real 'you,' is spirit.

In John 3:3-13, God gives us a picture of the triune nature of man. In these passages of scripture, when Jesus responded to Nicodemus' statement that, He, Jesus, must have come from God because of the miracles He had performed. Jesus responded to Nicodemus by stating; *"That which is born of the flesh is flesh and that which is born of the Spirit is spirit," John3:6,* at first glance this quote from Jesus appears to be just an explanation about only the body and the spirit. However, the soul is implicated in that dialogue. When Jesus was teaching Nicodemus about the body and spirit and the need for a person to be born-again, He did not need to talk about the soul because Nicodemus himself was the 'soul' who was receiving the teaching from Jesus. Jesus was talking to Nicodemus' soul; his consciousness/mind, that part of him that was trying to reason (reasoning takes place in the soul) and make sense of what Jesus was saying to him about being born-again of the spirit.

This great teacher of Israel and the Law was trying desperately to understand what Jesus was saying to him. However, since Nicodemus' spirit was not born-again, because Jesus had not yet been crucified, resurrected, ascended, and had not yet sent the Holy Spirit, his mind and reasoning capabilities were unable to understand the spiritual truths of what Jesus was saying. It was clear that Nicodemus was spiritually dead, and in his 'natural' state, and that he needed to be born-again for him to truly understand what Jesus was saying to him, but how could he? Jesus had not yet been crucified and resurrected and the Holy Spirit had not yet come.

In Nicodemus' 'natural' state, it was impossible for him to understand the reality of what Jesus was saying. *"For what man knows the things of a man except the spirit of the man which is in him? Even so **no one knows the things of God except the Spirit of God**. Now we have received, not the spirit of the world, but the Spirit who is from God, **that we might know** the things that have been freely given to us by God. These things we also speak not in words which man's wisdom teaches but which the Holy Spirit teaches, comparing spiritual things with spiritual. "But the **natural man** does not receive the things of the Spirit of God, for **they are foolishness to him; nor can he know them, because they are spiritually discerned,"** 1 Corinthians 2:11-14.*

It is obvious that there could be no spiritual discernment or understanding from Nicodemus, due to the fact, that the ultimate sacrifice of Christ had not taken place. Jesus had not ascended into heaven and the Holy Spirit had not yet been given. The obvious outcome was rather than ascending to the higher reality of the spirit, which was impossible for him to do, Nicodemus' reasoning naturally descended to the lower realities of the body or the physicality of the material world, rather than the spirit. He tried to reason the idea of being 'born-again' as re-entering the mother's womb, in order, to experience the second birth.

Jesus, fully aware of Nicodemus' inability to grasp the profoundness of what He was saying to him, said to Nicodemus; *"Are you the teacher of Israel and do not know these things?" John 3:10 (NKJV).* This is a rhetorical question for Jesus was fully aware that Nicodemus could not understand the full implication of what He was revealing to him, however,

Jesus also knew, with complete certainty, that this exchange of words, would be written down as His word for us to read today.

My hope is that as you read through this book you will gain a fresh new insight into the truth of God's word as it pertains to the actuality of your new identity as a true child of God, born-again, precious in His sight, completely forgiven for every past, present and future sin.

You have been created in Christ Jesus to attain the glorious riches of Christ for all eternity as you grow in grace and in the knowledge of Him. You will begin to see that you are free from all condemnation, as you begin to understand the realities of what Jesus has already done for you, and continues to do for you, on a daily basis, until you are called home to be with Him, your true Lord and Savior. *"His divine power has given to us all things that pertain to life and godliness, through the knowledge of Him who called us by glory and virtue, by which have been given to us exceedingly great and precious promises, that through these you may be **partakers of the divine nature,**" 2Peter 1:3-4.*

As you read through this book you will notice that many of the scriptures that are dispersed throughout the book will be repeated many times in different contexts. This is due to the fact that God's word is able to clarify multiple topics, questions and inquiries about the reality of humanity and the invisible and visible world around us.

CHAPTER 1

THE PLAN

"In the beginning God created the heavens and the earth,"
Genesis 1:1.

There are only three categorical reasons why 'anything' exists. 'Anything' means just what is says, 'any-thing!' The first reason why something would exist is that it is eternal and has never not, not existed! It has always existed with no beginning and no end-eternal! This concept was, and is widely accepted by many scientist, who believed and still believe that the universe was and/or is eternal prior to the discovery of the cosmological Big Bang, which brought in the beginning of our universe and which now, not only gives certainty to the reality of the beginning of our universe, but also the implications that go beyond the mere material physicality of our perceived reality.

The second reason why 'anything' would exist is that it is self-created. The absurdity of this proposition should be obvious, however, a multitude of scientists along with many laypeople believe that this is possible, especially with the metaphysical and religious implications of the first reason. The absurdity of 'something' or 'existence,' creating itself out of 'nothing' or 'non-existence,' should be self-evident. This 'something' that comes from nothing would have to both exist and not exist at the same time and in the same sense, in order, for it to cause itself to come into existence-pure absurdity!

The third reason something would exist would be that it was created. We see this taking place every day. Some examples would be music, paintings, buildings, etc.... *"In the beginning God created the heavens and the earth," Genesis 1:1.* Several points that can be made about the above scripture are, 1.) There is a beginning to this universe (this is a known scientific fact). 2.) This universe; time (beginning), space (heavens), and matter (earth), was created. It is not eternal and did not spring forth, or emerge by itself from nonexistence and, 3.) God did the creating, not some kind of force or non-intelligent entity. At this point the question, 'Who then, created God?' must be addressed.

The first point to make is that God, by definition, is not created. If God was created, then whoever created Him, is the true God. However, we now have the beginning of an infinite regression of 'then who created Him... and Him...and Him. It appears that there doesn't seem to be an adequate answer to the question of who created God. The reason for his is that there cannot be an answer to an illogical and invalid question. Let me clarify this by restating the question using the phrase 'one-sided coin' or 'one-ended stick' instead of the word 'God.' If someone were to ask you who created a one-sided coin or where one could find a 'one-ended stick,' your answer should be, "there are no such things as 'one-sided coins,' or 'one-ended sticks,' they are an impossibility. In the same manner, there is no such thing as a created '*God*,' however, there are many created '*gods*.'

Created 'gods' can be found in the minds of authors who write fiction. The difference between a fictional god and a non-fictional God is that the fictional god is created from the mind of man, while from the non-fictional God comes the mind of man. Fictional gods make for great story-telling, while the one and only true God created men that can tell great stories.

The God that I am writing about is changeless, immutable and all knowing. There is nothing known that cannot be known by Him. He cannot come to know something, otherwise He would not be God. An all-knowing God cannot go from not knowing to knowing since He already knows all that could possibly be known. Since He created us, then that means He has known us and created us from the point of eternity, or his eternal mind.

God is eternal and resides in an eternal dwelling place. He has known us from the eternal, before the creation of the time-space-material universe, therefore, I have come from an eternal mind and, therefore, I am an eternal being, one with a beginning, but with no end. I will go to my eternal resting place where I will reside for all eternity. I am not eternal in the same sense as God is eternal; the uncaused cause, the necessary Being of all creation, one who has never not been. I, however, from the time God conceived me in His mind, became eternal or a never-ending being starting from the time of my existence in His mind. My decision to be with Him for all eternity is a freewill choice he has given me to make. My guess is that if you believe that God is created, then you have the wrong god! Not only the wrong god, but a non-existent false god!

So, what is God's purpose for giving us information about the beginning and the sustaining of the created universe with us in it? What is

God's reason for making known to us His thoughts about who we are, what we are, and why we are here? The very first verse in the Bible asserts that the heavens and the earth were created in the 'beginning.' This beginning is the beginning of space-time and matter-energy as we know it. This physical universe and all that is in it was created 'out of' something. This something that the universe comes 'out of,' comes out of the mind of God.

There are those that believe that the universe was brought into existence 'out of nothing.' Some atheist state that there was 'nothing' and somehow 'nothing' caused the universe to come into existence. The Bible does not state that God made the universe out of nothing, the mind of God is anything but 'nothing.' Whatever is in the mind of God is what actual reality is, as opposed to this temporal fading space-time and material-energy universe. This universe was brought into existence from God's spoken word. *"By faith we understand that the worlds were prepared by the **word of God**, so that what is seen was not made of things which are visible," Hebrews 11:3.* This scripture clearly teaches that the things that are seen or visible were made from something not seen or not visible.

Just because something is not visible does not mean it does not exist. Gravity and the electromagnetic force are invisible, yet we know they exist. If you have never thought about the unseen world, think about the fact that you have never seen your mind, and yet I doubt that you believe you don't exist. If you have any doubt as to the existence of your own mind, as some atheist assert, just ask yourself, who is doing the doubting? Rationally speaking, there is nothing in this physical universe that can create itself. As stated above, the idea that the universe can create itself is an absurdity, no matter how many minds believe that to be the case.

From the Biblical perspective, the universe had a beginning and, as we now know, the entire universe is winding down (Law of Entropy) and therefore, it is not eternal. As believers in Christ we believe that the universe and all that is in it was created by the eternal mind of God, which sprang forth God's entire plan for mankind from beginning to end, using only the power of His word (Jesus). *"He is the image of the invisible God, the firstborn over all creation. For **by Him all things were created** that are in heaven and that are on earth, visible and invisible, whether thrones or dominions or principalities or powers. **All things were created by Him.** And He is before all things, and in Him **all things consist**,"* Colossians 1:15-17.

This coming forth of all creation came forth from the immaterial omniscient *mind of God* without the use of any kind of preexisting space or matter and entails the creation of the unseen invisible spiritual world and the visible material physical world, as well as the world systems that are in power. God, who knows the beginning from the end, knows it without error; fully and completely, lacking absolutely nothing in all that He knows or can be known about everything there is to know in the past, present, future and/or the eternal. God's blue-print or idea of the unseen heavenly spiritual world, the universe, humanity and its world systems are an idea that is total and absolute in its perfection from beginning to eternity.

As humans, we understand the concept of planning a big event such as a wedding. It is a natural human function and experience to conceptualize an idea, and then engage our minds in the exercise of planning it from beginning to end so that our ideas become actualized. Since we live in a space-time continuum, our conceptualizing, creating and bringing about our immaterial ideas into this physical realm, they must pass through the window of time. From their inception, our 'ideas' undergo the process of springing forth from a thought in our minds to the final material or immaterial reality they become, such as the material of this book and the immaterial message that is conveyed in this book. Both must pass through time and be presented materially in print, on a computer, in a book or some other form of auditory, tactile or visual media.

An idea goes from its potentiality in the mind to its actualization in the real world. Much is left to be done in the intermediate stage of how an idea comes to be actualized. The intermediary work of an idea must first take into account all contingent and possible barriers that might impede its realization. This is in its most basic form, how human agency brought into existence and continues to bring into existence, the civilization we live in; cities, roadways, buildings, etc.

Humanity's method of bringing things into existence is the same as Gods in that, mind precedes matter. The difference is that God creates matter that did not exist, and humans create with matter that is already existent. In the temporal realm, the immaterial idea is first conceived in the mind of its creator and then becomes what it is intended to become through the process of time, using materials within the confines of space. Both material (buildings) and immaterial (music) ideas are first created in the mind.

In like manner, you were first created in God's mind before you or our visible and invisible creation were spoken into existence. That means that the created universe was created with you in mind for an eternal purpose, rather than you just being a by-product of the forces of nature, as atheist would have you believe. Have you ever had an imaginary friend, or conjured up an imaginary person in your mind? For instance, the man or woman of your dreams, or your first child and wondered what they would be like or even what you would like them to be like, or look like? If you can grasp this concept, then think about the fact that that is who you are! The person God thought up in His mind that ended up being you!

God's power is infinite, He, therefore, can cause to come into existence, whatever He thinks up in His mind. He is also a benevolent all-loving God and whatever He creates, He creates out of absolute love for the thing He creates. What we need to do is put the creation of this world into perspective. We need to understand that this created universe and all that is in it, is *not the 'end-result'* of God's plan. It is only a stepping stone to an incomprehensible, blissful, loving, infinite, intimate, relationship with the creator of all things, in a kingdom that is infinite in every possible way imaginable and beyond imaginable. God's plan is a plan of procession that is in the process of doing exactly what He planned it to do. Part of God's perfect plan are the imperfections of this temporal existence, which is purposed for His final perfect state. He knows all things and there is nothing that exists that He is not totally and completely aware of, for He knows all things from their beginning and to their end, (read Job chapters 38 & 39 in their entirety).

God's creation of the universe and mankind is at this point in time, in its absolute perfect state that it is intended to be. It may not be in the state that we would like it to be, but then again, we are not the Creator of all creation. Mankind is not an unexpected freak of nature, nor is mankind in the process of undertaking plan 'B' because plan 'A' was somehow thwarted by an unexpected intrusion into God's eternal plan of salvation for mankind by angelic or human beings.

God's plan of salvation for mankind through Jesus Christ is not a necessary afterthought that needed to be interjected to save the anticipated human race from Adam and Eve's defiance in the Garden of Eden. Nor is the human-race a second choice for God to pick from after Lucifer and the angels fell. God created the angelic host knowing that Lucifer would fall and take a portion of the angels with him. His plan did not need to be thought out from beginning to end or have contingencies in place, as well as, have an alternate plan in case things went awry. His plan is the perfect eternal plan, which contains the best of all possible world scenarios for Him to bring to fruition His purpose - YOU! Yes, you are His purpose. He freely and intentionally created the universe and humankind, to bring into existence a people to call His own.

The consummation and fulfillment of God's plan will take place at the end of the age when God puts to end this temporal reality with His eternal reality. Part of that fulfillment is when we depart from this physical world and awaken in the arms of our Lord and Savior. The point of conversion, or when we are born-again, is the beginning of our salvation. The intermediary stage of our salvation takes place after our conversion and continues until the point of physical death in this material world. The *intermediary stage of salvation* or the point right after our conversion deals with the sanctification of our soul, or in other words, the renewing of our; consciousness, desires, thoughts, intentions, etc.... *"And do not be conformed to this world, but be transformed by the **renewing of your mind,** that you may prove what is that good and acceptable and perfect will of God, "Romans 12:1.* This intermediate stage that is taking place in our soul (consciousness/mind) is a lifelong endeavor that is being molded towards good works that God has prepared for us to accomplish, *"For we are His workmanship, **created in Christ Jesus for good works**, which God has prepared beforehand, **that we should walk in them,**' Ephesians 2:10.*

Because we have been created in Christ Jesus, our born-again spirit, which has been infused with God's Holy Spirit, not only confirms in our mind, through the study of His word, the knowledge of His will for us, but also enables us to perform His will. Upon hearing the good news of Christ Jesus, those who would receive Him as their Lord and Savior will be become God's children and will receive an inheritance and rewards beyond humanities ability to comprehend the full treasures of His gifts, while here on earth. This starts with the infilling of the Holy Spirit at the point of conversion and culminates with born-again believers taking on His divine nature in heaven.

Imagine that! We will take on the nature of God. *"Grace and peace be multiplied to you in the knowledge of God and of Jesus our Lord, as His divine power has granted to us all things that pertain to life and godliness, through the knowledge of Him who called unto his own glory and excellence, by which He has granted to us His precious and very great promises, so that through them* **you may become partakers of the divine nature,** *having escaped from the corruption that is in the world because of sinful desire."* 2 Peter 1:3-4. *"Beloved, now* **we are children of God;** *and it has not yet been revealed what we shall be, but we know that when He is revealed,* **we shall be like Him,** *for we shall see Him as He is,"* 1 John 3:2. Yes, we will take on His divine nature! No longer will we be what we are now, nor will we be constrained by the physicality and darkness of this world, but instead we will be released from every constraining obstacle known to mankind.

The end result of man's salvation is not just to be saved, or to make it into heaven, rather, it is the intimate union of man's spirit with God's Holy Spirit. *"I do not pray for these alone, but also for those who will believe in Me through their word; that they* **all may be one,** *as You, Father, are* **in Me,** *and* **I in you; they may be one in Us...I in them and You in Me,** *that they may be made* **perfect in one***..." John 17:20-23.*

God's plan, as stated in the Bible, is for everyone to step into eternity and be greeted by Him in the most loving compassionate way a person could possibly be greeted by another. His plan is for you to know that suffering, pain, anguish, sickness, greed, death, bills, schedules, deadlines, foreclosures, decay, cancer, rejection, poverty, disfigurement, everything bad, negative, etc.... are forever terminated and never to be experienced again.

Death here on earth is the end of this physical, material, and constraining suffering world. You, stepping into heavenly eternal bliss is the first eternal step, the first experience of the rest of your never-ending, infinite eternal life in God's kingdom that was created especially for you to freely enjoy, with your creator by your side for all eternity. God the Father of life, Creator and lover of your soul, Master and Creator of the visible and invisible kingdoms, He who freely gave us His Son, that we may partake of His divine nature and be one with Him as He is one with the Son for all eternity, plans for you to join Him.

CHAPTER 2

SIN: PART I

'Sin,' what is it? Understanding what sin really is makes all the difference, not only in the world, but in your life as well as in the heavenly realms. One thing that is obvious about sin is that it cannot be found on trees or under rocks. Sin is what is imbedded within the nature of man. Sin, within humanity, first manifested itself in the Garden of Eden when Adam and Eve willfully disobeyed God's command to not eat of the tree that God had told him not to eat from. Imagine that, probably thousands of trees that Adam could eat from except one, and he had to eat from the one he was told not to eat from. Adam sinned because the capacity or ability to sin was inherent in Adam as well as within Eve's spirit. When God created Adam and Eve, He created them with 'freewill.' The ability to choose right from wrong, to decide to do or not do, to accept or reject whatever one wants to accept or reject. This includes believing in Him and accepting His provision for salvation or rejecting Him and His provision for salvation. Whenever someone does something that is against God's will, that person is sinning.

Sin is a force within us that moves us to do what we want to do, when we want to do it, for the pleasure of experiencing what it is we want, when we want it. When God created water, He created it with the purpose of water sustaining life to living things, but He also knew that water would 'wet' whatever it touches. Water cannot not wet things. Sin in humanity is like wetness is to water. You cannot touch water without getting wet, wetness is the natural result of being touched by water. In the same way, there can be no such thing as *sin* in this physical universe unless humanity exists.

Sin is not just the act of doing something someone should not do or abstaining from doing something someone should do. Sin resides within the immaterial soul and spirit. It is an inherent and intrinsic immaterial force or law, with the power to exert is *lust* or *want,* at all times, and with such force, that it will at times extinguish or annihilate anything in its path that may thwart its goal of attainment.

Sinful behavior is only the outward external manifestation of an inner force. From the time we are born, to the time we enter the grave, we are constantly moving towards attaining something, whether it be something as simple as eating a piece of candy or committing a heinous crime, to fulfill a wanted desire such as acquiring one's illegal drug of choice.

The manifestations of sin are clearly seen by the outward acts people commit. Everyone sins easily and daily. As a matter of fact, sinning is part of God's plan. That may sound strange, but let us look at the following scriptures, *"For you were once disobedient to God, yet have now obtained mercy through their (God is talking about the Jews here) disobedience, even so these* **(Gentiles or non-Jews)** *also have now been disobedient, that through the mercy shown you (Gentiles) they (Jews) also may obtain mercy. For* **God** *has* **committed them all to disobedience,** *that He might have* **mercy on all**, *Romans 11:30-32.* Who has 'committed all to disobedience? God has! Why did God commit everyone to disobedience? So, He could demonstrate His mercy! *"Moreover, the law entered that* **the offense might abound.** *But where* **sin abounded, grace abounded much more,** *so that as sin reigned in death, even so grace might reign through righteousness to eternal life through Jesus Christ our Lord, Romans 5:20,21.*

Who introduced the law to humanity? God did! Why did God introduce the law? That sin might abound! Why did God want sin to abound? So, He could demonstrate His grace! *"But the Scripture has* **confined all under sin,** *that the promise by faith in Jesus Christ might be given to those who believe,"* Galatians 3:22. Who confined 'all' under sin? God has confined everyone under sin! Why did God confine everyone under sin? To demonstrate to humanity, humanities inability to separate themselves from their intrinsic sinfulness. Another way to think of sin is to think of it as you would think of the force of gravity. The only way for gravity to exist is that there must be a physical material body such as the earth, the sun or moon, that causes gravity to exist.

In the same way, coming into this world with a physical material body and with an immaterial soul and spirit, causes sin to exist. In other words, being 'confined under sin' is the same as *being born into this world as a human being with a body, soul, spirit and a freewill that is 'dead to God.'* As stated above, when God created water he created it with the purpose of it giving life to living things, but He also knew that water would not only 'wet' whatever it touches, it would also destroy lives, homes and cities.

In the same manner when He created people, He did so with a purpose. Part of that purpose is for human beings to live life as imperfect people in an imperfect universe or to put it another way, to live sinfully in a sinful world at this specific point in time. As human beings we can procreate, but we can also terminate life. We are continually in a transactional state of; moving-resting, creating-destroying, buying-selling, giving-taking, working-playing, exfoliating-replenishing, laughing-crying, etc.

As human beings, we are always moving towards whatever it is that we desire to attain whether it be a better car, house, body, athletic ability, better physique, salary, job, etc. This process is always in a continual state of flux and disequilibrium and will remain so until we leave this world. While we live in this world we will naturally sin because it is within our God given nature to survive and in the process of surviving we sin.

In order to survive, we must not only do the things the body craves for, such as; food, water, warmth, coolness, sex, etc....but also the things that the immaterial soul craves for and is necessary for our existence such as; connectedness, love, the experience of creating, accomplishment, and competition. As human beings, we cannot help but sin during our physical, soul and spirit state while here on this earth. Our lives consist of living life in a physical universe with a physical body that contains a soul and spirit that are impregnated with a sinful, fallen nature.

Both the physical universe and the human beings that live within the physical universe are fallen and sinful. Both are sinful in that the composition of both are not the final state God has intended for the universe and humanity to be in, but are in the state God intended us to be *at this point in time* in history; *"For I consider that the sufferings of this present time are not worthy to be compared with the glory which shall be revealed in us. For **the creation** was **subjected to futility**, not willingly, but **because of Him who subjected it** in hope; because **the creation itself** also will be delivered from the bondage of corruption into the glorious liberty of the children of God. For we know that **the whole creation groans and labors** with birth pangs together until now. Not only that, but we also who have the first fruits of the Spirit, even **we ourselves groan within ourselves**, eagerly waiting for the adoption, **the redemption of our body**,"* Romans 8:18-23.

All born-again believers wait for the deliverance of the body from the 'bondage of corruption,' however, our *spirits* have already been delivered by the transforming power of God on the day we received Jesus as our Lord and Savior. Even though our spirit is transformed, we continue to live in our physical sinful body along with our sinful soul in this sinful, physical fallen world. The real you (spirit), however, is 'born-again,' and is now a *'new creation,'* therefore, sin no longer has a hold on you. This is because you (spirit) are removed from the penalty and power of sin even though the presence of sin is still within your body and soul and the world around you.

The problem of sin from a humanistic perspective is that everything about humanity is sinful and imperfect including our concepts, thoughts, feelings and/or our philosophy about sin. Our sinful mind can trick us into believing that there is either no such thing as sin or that others sin, and we don't or maybe we really aren't that bad when it comes to our sins. Think about the fact that the entire human race suffers because of one person eating a piece of fruit!? What is wrong about eating a piece of fruit or what is *sinful* about eating a piece of fruit? If you are a parent with children, then you have encountered this type of situation. The problem is not with the child eating a piece of fruit, but rather with disobeying the command to not eat the fruit, or the cake, or go outside, etc.

A young child cannot know or understand what is wrong with having a piece of candy, especially if that child *wants* that piece of candy when she *wants* it and she usually *wants* it now! If a child gets the opportunity to get what she *wants* when she *wants* it, her sinful nature will come into play and she will get what she *wants* when no one is looking. When that child grows up and has children of her own, she will know and understand why she must now take charge of her child's *wants and needs.* She knows that left to themselves, children will pick and do the wrong things, and in the process of doing something wrong they kill themselves, by accident. She *now* knows that when she was a child she was incapable of knowing and understanding the things that only adults can understand because they can only be understood once they are an adult.

In the same manner if a person is not born-again and filled with God's Holy Spirit and His word, then that person cannot know or understand the things of God, *"But the natural man does not receive the things of the Spirit of God, for **they are foolishness to him; nor can he know them,** because they are spiritually discerned,"* 1 Corinthians 2:14. Who is it that cannot receive the things of the Spirit of God? the natural man! The 'natural man' is the man who does not have the Spirit of God living in his spirit or in other words an 'unbeliever.' What are the 'things of God' to the natural man? They are *foolishness* to him. Not only are the things of God foolishness to him, he cannot even come to know them no matter the height of education, the depth of intellect or the width of philosophical understanding he may have.

Sin, which is not of God, is a concept not easily understood even though we engage in it and experience it daily. We can see the effects of sin and its' devastation in the world, whether someone wants to call it sin or not. People have suffered and died in the millions because of the sin of; greed, hatred, power, lust, jealousy, anger, revenge, pride, and so forth. As controversial as the concept of sin might be today, the concept of *sinless-ness,* which is of God, is a state that is completely foreign to all humanity.

To truly understand the concept of *sinless-ness* you must be *sinless,* but that seems to be an impossibility since everyone born into this world is born sinful and remains to be sinful until death. It is like telling a fish (if fish could understand human language) that the only way to be sinless is to be completely, totally, 100% dry! Another way to look at sin using the same 'sin = water' analogy is within the context of the law or the commandments of God. Sin is like the wetness of water and the law is like wearing a raincoat to protect yourself from getting wet, the problem is we cannot wear a raincoat 100% of the time and even if we could wear a raincoat 100% of the time we would still get wet when we drink water to stay alive, bathe, wash the dishes, etc.

On top of all that we are also made up of approximately 60% water. We cannot escape being wet inside and out, or in other words, like wetness, we cannot escape the presence and effects of sin. Sin is not only the manifestation of the means of getting what we want when we want it, as well as what we need, it is what is intrinsic within our material and immaterial composition. This is the situation God has deemed necessary for humanity.

What is of utmost importance, here at this point, is to understand, if we are going to grasp the reality of sin in the world and in our lives, that there are two types of sin.

The first type of sin is unforgivable sin, or 'sin unto death,' sin that we cannot even pray for. *"There is a __sin that leads to death__. I am not saying that you should pray about that. All wrongdoing is sin, and there is sin that does not lead to death,"* 1 John 5:16,17. This type of sin can only be committed by someone who does not have the spirit of God living in their spirit, whether they are religious or irreligious. *"He who is not with Me is against Me, and he who does not gather with Me scatters abroad. Therefore, I say to you, every sin and blasphemy will be forgiven men, but the **blasphemy against the Spirit will not be forgiven men**. Anyone who speaks a word against the Son of Man, it will be forgiven him; but **whoever**

speaks against the Holy Spirit, it will not be forgiven him, *either in this age or in the age to come," Matthew 12:30-32.* This first type of sin is the unforgivable sin-*blasphemy against the Holy Spirit.*

Obviously when you speak against someone you are not for them, you are against them. Speaking against the Holy Spirit and committing the unpardonable sin is not only speaking against the Holy Spirit, but also 'rejecting the *'free-gift'* of the Holy Spirit.' Rejecting the free-gift of the Holy Spirit is the ultimate insult to God, or the ultimate sin! This is so because of what it cost God to pay for the sins of the world through His Son, Jesus.

Jesus said that EVERY *sin* AND *blasphemy* against HIM will *be forgiven,* but anyone who speaks a word *against the Holy Spirit* **will not be forgiven.**

Jesus makes it very clear that ALL sins committed by anyone against Him will be forgiven (even by those who committed the sin of crucifying Him). These are the second type of sins, which are; 'forgivable sins.' 'Sins' against His perfect will, that are stated in the commandments and that are deep within our inner heart and mind, sins done by humanity to humanity, however, sin against God's Holy Spirit is unforgivable.

We must remember that Jesus took on human nature and was 100% human as well as 100% God. Humanity sinned against Jesus-the Man. That is why Jesus asked God the Father to forgive them (humanity) for crucifying Him; *"Father, **forgive them** for they do not know what they are doing," Luke 23:34.*

Those who crucified Him and those who watched were completely and totally unaware of who it was that they were really crucifying. Just like

Nicodemus, who could not understand the concept of being' born-again,' unless he was actually, 'born-again.' For God who knows even our darkest secrets these type of forgivable sins are no longer an issue, why? because; "*God was in Christ reconciling the world to Himself, **not imputing their trespasses to them, 2 Corinthians** 5:19.*

Those who reject the gospel message, reject the glorious, precious free-gift of the Holy Spirit, which leads to eternal damnation. There is no remedy for speaking against the Holy Spirit and therefore, that is why the scripture plainly tells us not to pray for that specific sin, the unforgiveable sin of rejecting the free-gift of the Holy Spirit. If you are inclined to believe that eternal damnation is a bit over the edge as a punishment for not wanting to receive this free-gift, then let me clarify what the 'free-gift' means, so we can understand why rejecting this gift is an eternal blasphemous sin.

We must first start with the reality that we do not have the power to create or annihilate ourselves. We may choose to end our life here on earth, however, that is only physical death and not annihilation. Annihilation is the total extinction of something, neither existing in this realm or in any other realm (spiritual or material). We are not on this earth by our choosing, nor can we choose to not exist. We may terminate our physical life here on earth, but we cannot cease to exist. We are spiritual-beings, that will exist for all eternity. Our condition, when we enter the human-race, is that of total depravity, not from our perspective but from God's holy and perfect perspective.

God has complete knowledge and understanding of our 'sinful condition' when we are born into this sinful and fallen world. He is the author of our freewill and knows the sinfulness and enjoyment we get when we freely choose to sin. God also had the remedy for our situation and ordained it before He created this world. His plan to get us into heaven consists, in part, of us becoming like Him. We must partake of His divine nature for the purpose to be able to exist in the divine beauty and glory of the heavenly realms for all eternity. God, however, first had to become like us. God, had to partake of humanity, in order for Him to substitute our unrighteous sinfulness, for His perfect sinless-ness.

All humanity is sinful and cannot pay for its own sins, therefore, it is by necessity that only a sinless person is qualified to make the substitutionary transaction. Only someone outside the mix of sinful humanity in a fallen universe, is capable to make the transaction. Trying to pay for our sins is like saying to a Loan Shark; 'Hey, can I borrow some money to pay off what I owe you?' It is logically, rationally and physically impossible to pay for our own sins.

Jesus, the Son of God, had to cease being who He was prior to the incarnation, in order, to become one of us. He left his throne in the heavenly realms to live in impoverished conditions in a body that now felt the weight of gravity, weather, sickness, pain, etc. Yet that is nothing compared to the brutal and *voluntary* horror and pain of the beating He had to endure prior to the crucifixion, the pain of the actual crucifixion; the physical, emotional, mental anguish while hanging on the cross with nails driven through His body and a crown of thorns on his head. As horrific as that sounds, it does not come close to the humanly incomprehensible pain he experienced when he became the sin of the world, which led to the total separation of God the Father from His presence.

No person in the history of creation will ever endure what Jesus had to endure just so we can 'freely' go to heaven. He, without a doubt, is a 'free- gift' for us from God, but it cost Him dearly. Not only did it cost Him dearly, Jesus paid the price with joy knowing that **we** would be redeemed from this fallen world, that **we** will (if **we** choose Jesus) spend eternity with Him in paradise. That is why rejecting the 'free-gift' of the Holy Spirit is sinful, blasphemous and _unforgivable_. The consequences are eternal and damning, but the rewards for accepting this precious free-gift are never ending bliss in the heavenly realms for all eternity. All other sins be them; lying, cheating, adultery, fornication, and yes, even murder, are forgivable when we turn to Christ and believe in Him as our Lord and Savior. Yes, we will be cleansed and remain spiritually cleansed from all unrighteousness, however, where does one go when they reject the creator of all life?

No one can save themselves from physical death, much less spiritual death, which is total, absolute separation from God for all eternity! You had no say so in being brought into this existence, but you do have a say so, as to where you want to spend your, never ending existence; in heaven or hell. Today all unbelievers have only one command; Get saved!! *"I have set before you, life and death, blessing and cursing; therefore, chose life, that both you and your descendants may live;"* Deuteronomy 30:19. *"Most assuredly, I say to you, unless one is* **born again**, *he _cannot see the kingdom of God_,"* John 3:3.

What God the Father has done for humanity through His Son Jesus is set up humanity like it was for Adam and Eve in the Garden of Eden. Adam and Eve also had only one command to follow, *"You may surely eat of every tree of the garden, but of the tree of the knowledge of good and evil you shall not eat,"* Genesis 2:15-17 (ESV). That's it, only one command, they failed and fell from grace and sin crept in, or did sin creep in? No, sin was already within them, within their soul, in their *freewill to choose,* the potential to sin lay within their consciousness.

Any creature created by God that is conscious of its own consciousness and that possesses a freewill to choose to obey or disobey God, will choose both. It is within the nature of a conscious creature to do all that is possible for it to do. If God created humans with the ability to fly and flying was a sin, humans indubitably would fly. God created Adam and Eve with the potential to sin with full omniscient knowledge that they would sin and fall from grace into this sinful earthly world. The great news is that God has, through the sacrifice of Jesus-for the removal of the sins of the world, placed all humanity in the same situation as Adam and Eve, *"Behold the Lamb of God, who takes away the sins of the world, John 1: 29.*

Jesus has taken away and more accurately, He has atoned for the sins of the world and left us with one command-*get saved!* If you accept God's one and only begotten Son as your Lord and Savior (eat of the tree of life; Jesus!). You will *immediately* be delivered from the kingdom of darkness and placed into His heavenly kingdom, *"for He has delivered us from the domain of darkness and transferred us to the kingdom of His Beloved Son, Colossians 1:13 (ASV).* If that sounds too simplistic, sorry! It is! All a person needs to do is believe Jesus is the Savior of the world, repent of their sins and receive Him as your Lord and Savior and you are saved for all eternity.

What many people do not realize is that their sinful behavior is not what keeps them from entering the kingdom of heaven and spending eternity with God. It is their rejection of the free-gift of God's Holy Spirit. *"...it is to your advantage that I go away, for if I do not go away, the Helper will not come to you; but if I depart, I will send Him to you. And when He comes, He will **convict the world of sin,** and of righteousness, and of judgment: **of sin,** because they **do not believe in Me**; of righteousness, because I go to My Father and you see Me no more; of judgment, because the ruler of this world is judged, John 16:7-11.*

Why was Jesus telling His disciples that it is to their advantage that He goes away? So, He could send the Helper, the Holy Spirit of God. What is one of the purposes of the Holy Spirit? To convict the world of sin! What is this great sin (singular) that the Holy Spirit will convict the world of, as stated above? Rejecting the free-gift of the Holy Spirit, which amounts to 'Unbelief,' or as scripture states; *"And when He has come, He will convict the world of **sin**, and of righteousness, and of judgment: **"of sin** because they **do not believe in Me**." John 16:8,9.* That's it! Jesus said it over and over during His ministry when He graced the world with His presence here on earth. *"And as Moses lifted up the serpent in the wilderness, even so must the Son of Man be lifted up, "that **whoever believes in Him** should **not perish** but **have everlasting life.** "For God so loved the world that He gave His only begotten Son that **whoever believes in Him** should **not***

perish *but* ***have everlasting life.*** *"For God did not send His Son into the world to condemn the world, but that the world through Him might be saved.* *"****He who believes*** *in Him is* ***not condemned****; but he who* ***does not believe is condemned*** *already, because he has* ***not believed*** *in the name of the only begotten Son of God," John 3:14,18.*

Notice that those who *do not believe* in Him are already condemned, but those who believe in Him are *not condemned*. The sin of the world is humanity not having the Holy Spirit living inside their spirit or in other words, not being 'born-again.' The penalty for rejecting the free-gift of the Holy Spirit is total separation from God for all eternity. The separation from God for all eternity is not contingent on your behavior, whether it is sinful or righteous, but rather because a person cannot enter a different kind of dimension unless they are created specifically for that dimension. That is what being born-again is all about, it is about becoming a *'new creation.'* It is not about going from sinning to not sinning. That is an impossibility for mankind and God knows it.

No one in this universe can get away from or cease from sinning. We can choose to not sin, sin less often, and even stop sinning for a while, but we can never come to a point, while in this physical body in this physical world, of annihilating all sin from our physical and mental life (our spirit is another matter). However, believing in Jesus takes away the *penalty* and *condemnation* of sin, even when we do sin. *"If we say we have no sin we deceive ourselves, and the truth is not in us," 1 John 1:8, "My little children, these things I write to you, so that you may not sin. And* ***if anyone sins, we have an Advocate with the Father, Jesus Christ*** *the righteous," 1*

*John 2:1, "There is therefore now no **condemnation** for those who are in Christ Jesus. "For the law of the Spirit of life has **set you free** in Christ Jesus from **the law of sin and death**," Romans 8:1,2 (ESV).*

'Believing' **in** Christ Jesus is how someone is not only cleansed from all their sins, but how one remains, in their *spirit*, continually clean, pure, perfect, sanctified and holy. When a person believes in Christ and receives Jesus as their Lord and Savior, their **spirit** is *born-again* and placed in the heavenly realms, *"But God, who is rich in mercy, because of His great love with which He loved us, even when we were **dead in trespasses**, made us alive together with Christ (by grace you have been saved), and raised us up together, and **made us sit together in the heavenly places** in Christ Jesus," Ephesians 2:4-6.*

Every born-again believer is **in** Christ Jesus as Christ Jesus is **in** them as He is in God the Father. *"I do not pray for these alone, but also for those who will believe in Me through their word **(the Bible);** that they all may be one, as You, Father, are **in** Me, and I **in** You; that they also may be one **in Us**...I **in** them, and You **in** Me, that they may be made perfect in one," John 17:20,21,23.* This spiritual transformation of a born-again believer's spirit in becoming one with Jesus and God the Father is an event that is accomplished by God for the purpose of guaranteeing not only a person's salvation for all eternity, but also for the reward or inheritance they will receive in heaven. *"In Him you also trusted, after you heard the word of truth, the gospel of your salvation; in whom also having believed, you were **sealed with the Holy Spirit of promise,** who is the **guarantee of***

our inheritance, until the possession, to the praise of His glory."
REWARDS!!!

CHAPTER 3

SIN: PART II

THE THIEF

The story of the two thieves who were crucified alongside Jesus, is one of the most profound and illuminating stories in the Bible. The truth of these scriptures demonstrates the love, grace and forgiveness of God. It also demonstrates the incomprehensibleness of the width, depth, length and height of the greatest sacrifice in the history of all creation, as well as the end-result of the thieves who were within a breath's distance of the creator of the universe. One thief made it into heaven and one lost his very soul. This story in my estimation, dispels many theological religious superstitious, false precepts, ever concocted by man, about some of the irrational religious requirements and traditions of men preached to people as to what is needed to get saved.

The truth of the scriptures in the gospel of Luke portrays two thieves who were obviously the worst of the worst who had been caught for their crimes and sentenced, crucified and left to die on the cross. *"There were also two others, criminals, led with Him to be put to death. And when they* *had come to the place called Calvary, there they crucified Him, and the criminals, one on the right and one on the left. Then Jesus said, "Father, forgive them, for they do not know what they do." And they divided His garments and cast lots. And the people stood looking on. But even the rulers with them sneered, saying, "He saved others, let Him save Himself if He is the Christ, the chosen of God." The soldiers also mocked Him, coming and offering Him sour wine, and saying, "If You are the King of the Jews, save Yourself." "And an inscription also was written over Him in letters of Greek, Latin, and Hebrew: THIS IS THE KING OF THE JEWS. Then one of the criminals who were hanged blasphemed Him, saying, "If you are the Christ, save Yourself and us." But the other, answering, rebuked him, saying, "Do you not even fear God, seeing you are under the same condemnation? "And we indeed justly, for we receive the due reward of our deeds; but this Man has done nothing wrong." Then he said to Jesus, "Lord, remember me when You come into your kingdom." And Jesus said to him. "Assuredly, I say to you, **today you will be with Me in Paradise,"** Luke 23:33-43.*

The remarkable thing about the truths in these scriptures, is the fact that, although both criminals are guilty, justly paying for their crimes and are at death's doorstep, one of them enters paradise with Jesus Himself! When Jesus responded *"Assuredly, I say to you, today you will be with me in paradise,"* to the thief, who asked only to be remembered, Jesus did not ask the thief to do or say anything! There is no mention in scripture of Jesus telling the thief he had to do, or say anything, to get into the kingdom of God. Jesus did not need to tell the thief to do anything, because the thief said all he had to say to get into the kingdom of God.

Remember when Jesus was at the well and asked the Samaritan woman for a drink of water (John 4:7-18). He told, the woman at the well, her life story concerning the men she had had in her life, to which she stated to the other Samaritans, *"Come, see a Man who told me all things that I ever did. Could this be the Christ?" Luke 4:29.* Jesus could have told the thief all the criminal and sinful acts he ever did and then tell him, 'confess all your sins to me now before you die,' or He could have said, 'sorry, but you are the worst of the worst and you are not worthy to enter the kingdom of God.'

Jesus also could have mocked the thief and told him that if he could get off the cross, stop stealing, go to church, be baptized, give to the poor, repent of all his sins, be an upright outstanding citizen, then he could possibly be considered 'good enough' to make it into God's kingdom. Instead, Jesus tells the thief, "Assuredly, I say to you, *today* you will be with Me in Paradise." What? How in heaven's name did this despicable, lowly, worthy of a crucifixion criminal, make it into heaven with Jesus?

The other important thing to remember is that Jesus said "today." He did not say tomorrow or later or after a time, no He said, "today." That removes all concepts of there being 'some kind' of 'holding place' where one can still hope to get into heaven if others 'pray hard enough' for him, or in other words, there is no 'purgatory.'! *"And as it is appointed for men to die once, but after this the judgment,"* Hebrews 9:27. One thing is for certain, this thief did not have the opportunity to do anything to get himself into heaven, he had absolutely nothing he could offer God to get himself into heaven and if he did, how could he? I think we could surmise that the thief had nothing, could do nothing and had done nothing to get into heaven. But there he is, in heaven, as you read this, he is enjoying the reality and blissfulness of heaven. How about the other thief? How about the soldiers or the rulers who crucified Him or those standing and watching?

If you notice that in these passages of scripture, there are seven dialogues taking place; 1.) Jesus speaking to His Father; *"Father, forgive them, for they do not know what they do,"* 2.) the rulers who said; *"He saved others, let Him save Himself **if** He is the Christ, the chosen of God."* 3.) the soldiers speaking to Christ and mocking Him, saying; *"**If** you are the King of the Jews, save Yourself."* 4.) One of the thieves speaking to Jesus who 'blasphemed' Jesus stating; ***"If** you are Christ then save us and yourself,"* 5.) the thief speaking to and rebuking the other thief for not fearing God; *"Do you not even fear God, seeing you are under the same condemnation? "And we indeed justly, for we receive the due reward of our deeds; but this Man has done nothing wrong."* 6.) The same thief who rebuked the other thief and then speaks to Jesus; *"Lord, remember me when You come into your kingdom,"* and finally; 7.) Jesus speaking to the thief that addressed Him as Lord and who asked only to be remembered, stating; *"Assuredly, I say to you, **today you will be with Me in Paradise.**"*

In the gospel of Luke and in the gospel of John, throughout all *this dialogue* in this horrific scene, Jesus speaks to only four persons. His mother to whom He stated, "Woman, behold thy son," and another disciple to whom He stated, "Behold, thy mother." The other two persons addressed by Christ Jesus Himself at the greatest point of all creation-the crucifixion of the one and only begotten Son of God, the Son of Man, the Creator of all creation, who is dying for the sins of the world are, God the Father and the thief. This is just unbelievable, on one side we have the righteous, holy omnipotent, omnibenevolent GOD of heaven, His mother and one of His close disciples and on the other side we have a thief! A rotten, low-life, scum of the earth who has more than likely devastated many lives and livelihoods because of his thievery. The contrast is staggering! He spent no time or breath on the rulers, the soldiers or even the other thief.

The word 'if' plays an important part in these scriptures. 'IF,' spoken by the rulers, soldier and unrepentant thief in their remarks towards Jesus, evidenced the lack of belief in Jesus as Lord and Savior of all creation. Their remarks were sarcastic, crass, demeaning and void of any sincere belief that Jesus was who He said He was. Jesus knew that in their hearts there was no repentance and absolutely no belief that He was the Christ, they had no belief that He could save them from their sins. The other thief, however, spoke from his heart and demonstrated his belief that Jesus was Lord, not of this world and going back to His kingdom. At this point it is important to note that both thieves, the soldiers, the rulers, the people standing watching as well as the whole world were forgiven for their sins. *"Father, forgive them, for they do not know what they do."* Who did Jesus ask God the Father to forgive? *'Them'!* Who is 'them,'? Humanity is 'them,' we are 'them.' The sins of the world were taken away upon His death on the cross, *"Behold the Lamb of God who **takes away the sin of the world**, John 1:29.* Why then did the unrepentant thief not make it into Paradise with Jesus and the other thief that Jesus stated would be with Him in Paradise? His sins were also forgiven, were they not? Yes, his sins were forgiven along with the sins of the world. His sins were not held against him. Then why didn't he make it into Paradise? Because having your sins forgiven by the sacrifice of Jesus on the cross is only the first part of God's deal with humanity.

The second part of the deal is you *believing* that the first part of the deal is absolute truth, or in other words you must come to the point that by faith, based on the evidence of God's Holy word (the Bible), you *believe* and put your trust (second part) in Christ Jesus as your Lord and Savior. That is why the unrepentant thief did not make it into Paradise with Jesus. His sins were forgiven but he was *not repentant* and did *not believe* that Jesus was who He claimed to be. We are like those thieves in that there is absolutely nothing we can do or give to get ourselves into heaven apart from God's grace.

You, however, may think that we are nothing like those thieves, but think again. We are bound hand and foot, disabled, incapacitated, and at death's doorstep every second of everyday without the ability for us to get ourselves out of this fallen state and into a perfect, sinless, unending, nonmaterial, spiritual world. Whether you care to think about it or not, someday you will die, maybe today, maybe tomorrow, or next maybe year, but the reality is that you and every person alive will someday die and there is nothing, absolutely nothing we can do about it, there is nothing we can do to stop death. When it comes to dying, we all are tied hand and foot.

The two thieves represent us, wherein one is a repentant person and the other is not, one is a believer and the other is not. Make no mistake about it, there is no middle ground with God. You are either with Him or against Him. The dialogue between the two thieves gives evidence that one of them remained unchanged in his heart and mind, not believing that Jesus was the Christ, the Son of God, while the other thief not only recognized his own depravity but also the sinless-ness and Lordship of Jesus. The fact that he called Jesus 'Lord' witnesses this fact. That thief also knew that Jesus was not of this world and was of another kingdom that was beyond the grave. If he had not believed that was so, he would not have said to Jesus, "Lord, remember me when you come into your kingdom." Why would the thief even ask Jesus to remember him? Both Jesus and the thief were hanging on a cross, death was immanent, there was no getting out of this one. The thief, however, knew something about this Man hanging on the cross next to him, He was no ordinary man.

Just like the woman at the well, Jesus not only knew the thief's immediate thoughts, but also his life story. Jesus knew that the thief believed in Him when he called Him Lord, and yet at the same time the thief knew he was not even worthy to be thought of as one that would be 'good enough' to get into heaven. *"For everyone practicing evil hates the light and does not come to the light, lest his deeds should be exposed. "But he who **does the truth comes to the light** that his **deeds** may be clearly seen, that they have been done in God," John 3:20, 21.* Coming to the light is 'doing the truth.' It is confessing with your mouth that Jesus is Lord, *"The word is near you, in your mouth and in your heart" (that is, the word of faith which we preach): that if you **confess with your mouth the Lord Jesus and believe in your heart that God raised Him from the dead**, you will be saved," Romans 10:8,9.*

This is how the thief was saved at the last moment of life here on earth. Well what about his 'deeds,'? Did he do any works for God? His deed or his work for God was *'believing'* in Jesus and he evidenced that *belief* when he called Jesus *'LORD,' "Do not labor for the food which perishes, but for the food which endures to everlasting life, which the Son of Man will give you, because God the Father has set His seal on Him."* Then they said to Him, *"What shall we do, that we may **work the works of***

God?" *Jesus answered and said to them, "This is the* **work** *of God, that you* **believe in Him,** *whom He sent," John 6:29.*

The thief also knew that Jesus would not die or at some point be raised from the dead, otherwise why would he ask Jesus; *"remember me when you get to your kingdom,"* while He hung there on the cross with him? If you are a believer, then one day you will meet the thief when you get to heaven and the most surprising thing will be that you will find out that you as well as any other person in heaven were not any better than that thief. You will also know that the thief is no longer a thief in heaven. His sins were completely washed away by the blood of Christ. The thief had believed in and was already forgiven before he died, that's how he got into heaven, by *believing* that Jesus was Lord, the Christ of God-not of this world!

Jesus was the first of the three to die and therefore, His departure from this world was the sure arrival of the Holy Spirit. We must remember that in God's heavenly realm there is no 'time,' so when Jesus takes His last breath, the Holy Spirit arrives at the scene. It is sort of like flipping a coin where when the head side of the coin is hidden from view, the tail side is immediately present. When the Holy Spirit arrives, guess who God's Holy Spirit arrives for? Our little scumbag thief! But how is this possible? Easy, his sins were not counted against Him because of what Christ Jesus' sacrifice was doing at that moment and consequently what His sacrifice did for the world, *"God was in Christ, reconciling the* **world to** *Himself,* **not imputing** *their trespasses to them," 2 Corinthians 5:19. "Blessed are those whose lawless deeds* **are forgiven,** *And whose* **sins are covered;** *Blessed is the man to whom the Lord shall* **not impute sin,"** *Romans 4:7. "Most assuredly, I say to you, he who hears My word and* **believes in Him** *who* *sent Me **has everlasting life**, and shall not come into judgment, but has **passed from death into life**, John 5:24. "I am the resurrection and the life. He who believes in Me, **though he may die, he shall live.** "And whoever lives and believes in Me **shall never die**," John 11:25,26.*

As is clearly depicted in the above scriptures, only through God's grace can we pass from immanent death into eternal life in heaven. A person can also reject God's grace and pass from physical death into eternal damnation. One thief received eternal life in heaven and the other, well, he did not!

"Again, the kingdom of heaven is like a merchant seeking beautiful pearls, who, when he had found one pearl of great price, went and sold all that he had and bought it," Matthew 13:45,46. Almost everyone that I have shared this scripture with and asked who they thought the Pearl of Great Price was, has answered; Jesus or God and that we are the merchant doing the seeking. That is what I myself use to believe until I heard a teaching by Derek Prince. How wonderful it is to have our eyes opened to God's truth and what a beautiful truth it is, let's look at this parable again, but this time let us preface it with the following scripture. *"As it is written: "There is none righteous, no, not one; There is **none who understands**; There is **none who seeks after God**. They have all turned aside; They have together become unprofitable; There **is none who does good, no, not one**..." Romans 3:10-12.*

Who is it that seeks after God? No one! That really means 'no one'! There is not one person who, not only does not seek after God, he has no understanding of the things of God. On top of all that there is *'no one'* who *does good, no not even one!* This is so because when we try to compare our goodness to God's goodness there is absolutely no comparison whatsoever. It is not even like comparing apples and oranges because both have some similarities in that both are fruit as well as physical objects in this physical world. God's goodness, holiness, righteousness, acts, thoughts, etc., are incomparable to the workings of human nature.

In the parable of the 'Pearl of Great Price,' it is the *kingdom of heaven* that is being allegorized and tells us that the kingdom of God is like a merchant out shopping for beautiful pearls. Apparently, this merchant is very rich, since he is out looking to buy beautiful pearls (plural), which we know are costly. In the process of time while looking for beautiful pearls, the merchant finds one of 'great price.' The scripture does not say, many pearls of great price, but 'one' of great price. The theological implication of this is extremely important. Understanding the significance of a singular pearl versus many pearls is the difference between eternity with God in heaven or eternity in 'the other place.' How so, you may ask? Well, a person cannot get into the kingdom of God through his affiliation, membership or any other group entity he or she may be associated with.

Salvation for all eternity commences with the belief in and acceptance of Jesus as our Lord and Savior and grows into a personal relationship between you and Jesus Christ. If you think that you're going to heaven because you are a Catholic, a Baptist, Amish, etc., Think again! Jesus said; *"Most assuredly, I say to you, unless **one** is **born again**, he cannot see the kingdom of God," John 3:3.* That is the criteria that is of eternal significance if we want to make it into God's heavenly kingdom. It must be a personal choice regardless of whatever affiliation one may be associated with.

We have in God's word a declaration of our human condition when it comes to God or the things of God. We cannot know them, nor do we even want to know them, much less seek them. *"But the natural man **does not receive** the things of the Spirit of God, for they are foolishness to him; **nor can he know them**, because they are **spiritually discerned,"** 1 Corinthians 2:14.* As stated above, if we are to receive and come to know the things of God, we must *first* be 'born-again,' therefore, clearly, we are not the merchant who seeks after God, who some think is the Pearl of Great Price.

Prior to God's grace intervening in our lives we had absolutely no inclination in searching for, much less selling all that we possess, to get to know God. A person may sell all he has, to buy a plot of land that he knows has oil, for financial gain, but selling all that he has for God for financial loss? For me that eliminates any human person being the 'Merchant.' The question then becomes, 'How is it that we are the 'pearl'? To answer that question, let's review what was stated earlier in this chapter by answering a few questions to help us understand the reality of the parable.

What did Jesus give up for Him to partake of humanity? In part, this is what He gave up; His infinite unrestricted spiritual body for a confined physical body, His intimate relationship with the Father and the Holy Spirit when the Father had to turn His back on Him when He was on the cross. His *original form* or spiritual composition as part of the trinity, when he became the *first* of the '*new creation*' that is marred for all eternity never to return to His condition prior to the incarnation. So, yes, Jesus sold all He had to buy that one 'pearl of great price' - You!

The reason the parable of the pearl is in this chapter is because, whether you agree or disagree, the *thief* is a 'Pearl of Great Price' to God. You are also a 'Pearl of Great Price,' to God. To God the Father, Jesus the Son and God's Holy Spirit, you are worth what Jesus went through to buy you back to God. He paid the full price for your spirit and soul that you may walk away from this sinful world into His heavenly arms that await you in heaven. You cannot work for it, buy it or earn it in any way, it is a free-*gift* of God!

CHAPTER 4

THE FLESH

"It is the spirit that gives life, the <u>flesh</u> profits nothing," John 6:63.

One thing that is explicitly clear in the Bible is the condition of, and the destiny of the actual physical fleshly body of a person. The condition of the human body is completely and absolutely, sinful in every way possible. It can never-ever know the things of the spirit. *For I know that **nothing good** dwells in me, that is in **my flesh**, Romans 7:18.* The flesh is that thing we carry around with us that allows our soul and spirit to remain in this physical universe. It is made up of matter that is animated by our soul and spirit. Matter that is made of particles, atoms and molecules that make up our cells which comprise our complete physical body.

Our physical body undergoes an ever-changing bio-physiological process that creates millions of new cells as millions of old cells die off daily. Our physical brain and body or 'the flesh,' as is sometimes depicted in the Bible, allows us to take in the stimulus of the world in which we experience life through the process of seeing, touching, tasting, smelling and hearing our surrounding environment. Our flesh is ever changing in its needs and wants, that is the nature of our flesh (as well as our soul).

The Bible is clear about the condition of the flesh, Jesus stated; *"It is the Spirit that gives life, the* **flesh profits nothing,***"* John 3:63. The physical fleshly body cannot profit anything spiritual, ever! You can beef it up, slim it down, coddle it, and even abuse it, but it will never reap anything of spiritual value. It is important to understand that our physical fleshly body does not give life to our soul or spirit, rather it is the spirit that gives life to the body and soul. Without the spirit, there is no life (being alive), without being alive/ spirit there is no soul and without the spirit/being alive, there is no body to move around in this physical world. Spiritual life is also eternal whether it be in heaven or in hell.

The flesh "profiting nothing" simply means that all things done by the flesh and to the flesh will never bring about any spiritual value (obviously when we do something for the Lord through the leading of the Holy Spirit we need to use our body to accomplish the work He has prepared for us to do, but the impetus to do so begins in our soul/mind after being 'born-again'). That is because our earthly fleshly body can never be regenerated, born-again or become a 'new creation,' and will inevitably return to the dust of the ground from where our bodies originated (physical matter), *"for dust you are, and to dust you shall return, "Genesis 1:19.*

In God's eyes, human flesh will not see immortality or in other words human flesh will not live within the heavenly realms, ***"flesh and blood** cannot inherit the kingdom of God, I Corinthians 15:50.* The interesting thing about the flesh is that the body, from the day of conception is in a continual state of flux and in the process and pathway of death. The cells that make up the body are infused with instructional information that communicate those instructions to other cells as they replicate exponentially, but only up to a certain point. The ratio of new cells replacing dying cells begins to diminish causing the body to go through the aging process up to the point of physical death. This is only the death of our earthly physical body.

In the Bible, the word 'flesh' has multiple applications. One application would be when Jesus stated; *"And unless those days were shortened, no **flesh** would be saved; but for the elect's sake those days will be shortened,"* Matthew 24:22. The word 'flesh,' being used by Jesus means, 'humanity' as a whole.

Another application of the word 'flesh' is used when referring to the natural state of an unregenerate person or the sin nature of an unsaved person, such as when Jesus asked His disciples; *"Who do men say that I, the Son of Man, am?* Peter replied, *"You are the Christ, the Son of the living God,"* Matthew 16:16. Jesus then stated to Peter; *"Blessed are you,*

Simon Bar-Jonah, for **flesh and blood** *has not revealed this to you, but My Father who is in heaven, Matthew 16:16-7.*

The word 'flesh' in this context is again referring to 'humanity,' as a whole or specifically to a human being (with a body, soul and spirit), who is an unsaved, unregenerate person, a person with the total absence and inability to conceive of, or utter anything truthful concerning the things of God. This type of flesh refers to the person who is a natural man with absolutely no spiritual discernment whatsoever, *"the natural man does not receive the things of the Spirit of God, for they are foolishness to him; nor can he know them, because they are spiritual discerned, 1 Corinthians 2:14.*

Peter's unregenerate fleshly nature (body-soul-spirit) was such, that he could, in no way, know that Jesus was 'the Christ, the Son of the living God,' unless God had revealed it to him. These scriptures give a clear picture of the condition of humanity at the time of Jesus' ministry while He was on earth. They tell us that no human, at that time before Jesus' crucifixion, resurrection, ascension and the infilling of the Holy Spirit, was capable of 'coming to know' the things of God on their own intellectual or intuitive power, but rather only by the power of God.

Only through the power of the Holy Spirit at the point of regeneration, or becoming born-again, is one able to comprehend the 'things of God'. Peter's statement, in the above scripture, where he proclaimed that Jesus was the Son of God, was uttered not by Peter's ability to discern spiritual truths, but rather, because God had revealed it to him at that specific time and for a specific purpose; that his response would be part of the writings of the New Testament for future believers to read. In this next scripture, *"And the Lord God caused a deep sleep to fall on Adam, and he slept; and He took one of his ribs and closed up the flesh in its place. Then the rib which the Lord God had taken from man He made into a woman, and He brought her to the man. And Adam said: "This is now bone of my bones and flesh of my flesh; she shall be called Woman, because she was taken out of a Man." Therefore, a man shall leave his father and mother and be joined to his wife, and they shall become one flesh, "Genesis 1:21-24.*

God is saying that once a man and a woman are united in marriage, they not only become one in the 'flesh,' when they share each other's fleshly body during the consummation of the marriage through sexual intercourse, but also throughout the continual commitment to one another, 'so as long as they shall live.' If taken literally, (as some take much of the Bible literally, that should not be taken literally, and without taking context into consideration), this passage of scripture would mean that the husband and wife become one conglomerate blob of flesh. This, however, is obviously not the case. What is not so obvious, as demonstrated by the enormity of divorces in the world, is the fact that God is talking about a covenant and intimate relationship between a man and a woman that should never be broken or violated.

"Now we know that whatever the law says, it says to those who are under the law, that every mouth may be stopped, and all the word may become guilty before God. Therefore, by the deeds of the law no flesh shall be justified in His sight," Romans 3:19,20. In the above passage, the word 'flesh,' has two different meanings, the first meaning deals with the

idea that no literal physical fleshly 'body' can be justified in God's sight, even if that person were to fulfill the entirety of the law, since the body is destined, by God, to never leave this earth, but will instead decay in the ground upon death.

The second meaning of the word 'flesh,' deals with the whole person; body, soul and spirit (flesh = person), an unregenerate person who is not born-again and is without the infilling of the Holy Spirit. This type of person has absolutely no hope, nor the ability to pull himself up from his bootstraps to make himself good enough to be justified in God's presence, again, even if he or she were to fulfill the entirety of the law. This passage declares that the physical fleshly body, or the law-abiding person, is totally worthless when it comes to the spiritual transformation one must undertake to know the spiritual truths of God.

The only thing a natural person can do with his or her fleshly body, is wear it, for he cannot be moved by the Spirit of God, in his 'non' born-again spirit, to decide in his soul, to carry out the things of God, in his body, that is an impossibility. The spiritual born-again believer, however, not only has the resources to carry out the things of God through the Holy Spirit living in his spirit, but also has the desire to carry out the true things of God. I state here, the 'true' things of God because there are many gods in the world and many religions in the world carrying out the things of their god(s), who are in reality, imaginary and false god(s). Again, it must be reiterated that we are a fleshly body, an immaterial soul and an immaterial spirit. It is our born-again God filled *spirit* along with our 'in the process of being sanctified-soul' that are *justified* upon salvation, not our body. So, although born-again believers have a fleshly body, their body will never be justified before God. Their 'born-again spirit' was justified by God at the point of conversion. As for the soul, the soul of a born-again believer is also justified before God at the point of conversion, but also goes through fluctuating back and forth between, either walking with the flesh (old-self, things of the world, demonic influences) or the born-again spirit (filled with God's Holy Spirit) and does so throughout their lifetime, but without condemnation from God. The born-again believer will mature and grow in God's grace to the degree they wish to grow, through the knowledge of Christ Jesus or become stunted in growth due to the lack of Biblical knowledge and Godly living.

This is the sanctification process that a believer is experiencing; fighting self, the world, and Satan, this is what Romans 7:1-25, is all about. It is about the believer's conflict with the regenerated born-again spirit that is attached to the conscious unperfected *soul/mind* of the believer that wrestles between doing the will of God, that is now knowable and doable, and what the fleshly body lusts for and has lusted for since birth.

Clarification is needed at this point about what the difference is between a believer sinning and a nonbeliever sinning? There is a vast difference! There are those that believe that born-again believers can fluctuate between being born-again, lose their salvation, get saved and then lose their salvation over and over again. This is because they do not understand the triune nature of man and the purpose and function of the body, the soul and the spirit.

This next scripture is an excellent example of the reality of not only the triune nature of man, but also the difference between a born-again believer and a non-believer. *"For those who live according to the flesh set their minds on the things of the flesh, but those who live according to the Spirit, the things of the Spirit. For to be carnally minded is death, but to be spiritually minded is life and peace. Because the carnal mind is enmity against God; for it is not subject to the law of God, nor indeed can be. So, then those who are in the flesh cannot please God,"* Romans 7:5-8.

Some believe that this scripture is talking about born-again believers switching back and forth between being carnally minded and spiritually minded resulting in being very displeasing to God. They think they are bad Christians and, therefore, struggle immensely with guilt and self-condemnation among other negative thoughts and emotions about themselves.

Let's revisit this scripture again, however, this time let us insert the words 'believer' and 'non-believer,' for the purpose of extrapolating the true meaning, which will help us understand more, the reality of our salvation and the reality of our triune nature. *"For those* (non-believers) *who live according to the flesh, set their* (non-believing soul) *minds on the things of the flesh* (body-world system)*, but those (born-again believers) who live according to the Spirit, the things of the Spirit. For to be carnally minded* (not saved, non-believers) *is death, but to be spiritually* (born-again in the spirit) *minded* (soul) *is life and peace. Because the* (non-believing) *carnal mind is enmity against God; for it is not subject to the law of God, nor* *indeed can be. So, then those* (non-believers) *who are in the flesh* (not saved-in the world) *cannot please God," Romans 7:5-8.*

What we really have here is scripture that declares to us the reality of how a non-believer is totally incapable of knowing, much less being led of the Spirit and a picture of a born-again believer who is capable of being 'spiritually' minded and able to be subject to the things of the Spirt of God. Now that we have had a closer and more in-depth look at this scripture, we can start to understand how it is that born-again believers can be both perfect and not perfect, sanctified and not sanctified at the same time.

A *non*-believer has a body-soul-spirit that are dead to the things of God. A born-again believer has a dead body, a soul that will always be in the process of being sanctified and a perfect spirit that is holy, perfect and sanctified. The body is needed to live in this physical universe, the soul/mind is needed to manipulate the body throughout this world and the spirit is what makes our body and soul live or be alive and is who believers really are. This will be a reoccurring theme throughout this book and an absolute necessity to understand if one is to grasp the reality of what God the Father, because of His great love for all humanity, has done through Jesus Christ. This includes the removal of all condemnation for those who trust in Christ.

What is also of utmost importance is to be able to grow in grace for the purpose of gaining the knowledge and wisdom of Christ and to know that God does not count your sins against you, *if* you have received Christ Jesus as your Lord and Savior; *"Blessed are those whose lawless deeds* *are forgiven, and whose **sins are covered**; Blessed is the man to whom the Lord shall **not input sin,**" Romans 4:7,8.*

Many Christians are leaving the faith or not sharing the gospel because they have come to believe that, as a born-again Christian, they must live a perfect life. They also know the sinfulness of their thoughts, words and deeds and walk around feeling condemned and guilty all the time. They think that this is just too hard a religion to try and keep, when in fact the opposite is true. In order to flesh-out (no pun intended) what is false from what is truth in our thinking, our first step is to consider our High Priest, *"who for the joy set before Him endured the cross,".....*"but He, having offered one sacrifice for sins for **all time**, sat down at the right hand of God,...For by one offering, He has **perfected for all time** those who **are sanctified**...their **sins and their lawless deeds I will remember no more**," Hebrews 12:1, 10: 12, 10:14, 10:17. "For in Him all the fullness of Deity dwells in bodily form, and in Him **you have been made complete** and He is the head over all rule and authority; and in Him **you were also circumcised with a circumcision made without hands, in the removal of the body of flesh** by the circumcision of Christ; having been buried with Him in baptism, in which you were also raised up with Him through faith in the working of God, who raised Him from the dead. And when you were dead in your transgressions and the uncircumcision of your flesh, **He made you alive together with Him**, **having forgiven us all our transgressions**, having **canceled out** the certificate of debt consisting of decrees against us and which was hostile to us; and He has taken it out of the way, having nailed to the cross." Colossians 2:9-13.*

If you are a born-again believer, then the above scriptures pertain to you. If you are a born-again believer, your flesh counts for nothing. The sins you commit *in the body or mind* are forgiven, covered, not held against you, because the real you is 'spirit.' The real you-spirit, 'cannot sin,' *"Whoever has been born of God **does not sin**, for **His seed <u>remains</u> in him**; and he <u>**cannot sin**</u>, because he has been **born of God**," 1 John 3:9.* You (spirit) are already in Christ and in the heavenly realms and therefore, God the Father, Jesus the Son and the Holy Spirit reside in your perfect sanctified **spirit!**

The meaning of being "circumcised with the circumcision made without hands, stated above," is the fact that God has separated the sinful physical body and soul from the Holy Spirit filled spirit, because of Christ's work on the cross and a person's belief in Him. Thus, the true self, the new creation or the spiritual born-again believer, walks in the newness of life with their physical body fighting the things of the spirit, while the soul (still sinful conscious-mind), decides, on a daily basis, who they will serve, the lust of their physical body and the world or their born-again Holy Spirit filled spirit.

Every born-again believer's spirit is in Christ as Christ is in the Father and as the Father is in Christ. Born-again believers are in Him as He is in them and therefore, they are also in the Father, even while our fleshly body is still walking around here on earth, see John 17:21-23. This is not a metaphor! Understanding that we are triune creatures and that our spirit is already in the heavenly realms is of utmost importance. It is also of utmost importance that we understand that we do not partake of the kingdom of heaven when we leave the confinement of this physical world.

The kingdom of God enters us the moment we receive Christ as our Lord and Savior. *"The kingdom of God does not come with observation; nor will they say, 'See here! or 'See there! For indeed, the kingdom of God is within you," Luke 17:20-21.* Make no mistake about it, the kingdom of God does not reside in our body nor within our soul as we will discover within the following chapters.

Dearly beloved, Jesus is risen!!! He is no longer on the cross and even though we know this as a historical fact, we sometimes lose sight of the reality of His resurrection, which is the focal point of our faith; that he died for our sins, but on the third day he rose from the dead! We must take Jesus off the cross and set our sights on the reality of Jesus sitting at the right hand of God the Father acting as our advocate, continuously, until we go home to be with Him for all eternity. We are to regard Christ in His new role, function and form sitting at the right hand of God doing what He went to the cross to do; sit at the right hand of God and intercede for us, on a daily basis. *"Therefore, from now on, we regard no one according to the flesh. Even though we **have known** Christ according to the flesh, yet **now** we **know Him thus no longer**." 2 Corinthians 5:16.*

CHAPTER 5

THE SOUL

"For the word of God is living and powerful, and sharper than any two-edged sword, piercing even to the division of soul and spirit," *Hebrews 4:12.*

When the Bible states that the 'word of God,' is 'able' to separate the soul from the spirit, it obviously means that those two aspects of the human composition can be separated. It also means that there must be a purpose for why God would want to separate them. In this chapter, we will learn the purpose of the soul and the reason it needs to be separated from the spirit. We know that God is a holy God and will not reside with sin, so it is difficult to imagine God's Holy Spirit living in our soul when we know that we have depraved and sinful thoughts, passions, and ideas that are conjured up intentionally as well as unintentionally through demonic and worldly forces that are continually around us.

If our soul and spirit are to be separated, as clearly stated in God's word, then I think it would be expedient for believers to know how this happens, when this happens and for what purpose this happens. Rather than conjuring up human speculations and theories without Biblical support, let us use scripture as a guide and as a pointer towards truth concerning the division of soul and spirit as clearly stated in Hebrews 4:12.

First, let's try and get a handle on the soul. The Soul consists of our mind, consciousness, freewill, desires, emotions, beliefs, and any other psychological, emotional and mental immaterial processes we engage in throughout our lifetime. 'Understanding' is a function of the soul/consciousness/mind. The ability for the soul to understand, is only possible if the person possessing the soul is 'alive,' to engage in any type of conscious reasoning process, or to put it another way, one must be spirit/alive, in order to possess a soul-consciousness-mind, that allows the person to engage in the process of; understanding, knowing, experiencing anything while moving about in the body in this physical world.

Our soul is that which is not 'physical' like the body, but is also *not* the spirit, however, it is immaterial like the spirit. It is the medium by which the body can be manipulated into doing what it is we want ('want' is in the soul) to do with our body, but it is also that entity that can choose not to do what the body lusts for through the help and leading of the Holy Spirit as well as through the disciplining of our wants and desires to match, what we as born-again believers know to be God's desires.

Since our soul does not go through the process of being 'born-again,' when we get saved, it always will be' in need of' Godly discipline, as will the body. Even though the soul and spirit are both immaterial, it is the spirit that is deemed perfect, sanctified and holy due to a person's belief in Christ, which in turn allows the spirit to be filled with God's Holy Spirit. When our soul and spirit are separated from our body upon death, our soul does *not* leave our spirit. When physical death takes place, a born-again believer's soul instantly becomes perfected, sanctified, holy and one with their spirit and with God the Father, Jesus the Son and the Holy Spirit. *"Sanctify them in truth; Thy word is truth. As thou didst send Me into the world, I also have sent them into the world. And for their sakes I sanctify Myself, that they themselves also may be sanctified in truth. I do not ask in behalf of these alone, but for those also who believe in Me through their word; that they may all be one; even as Thou Father, **art in Me**, and **I in Thee**, that **they also may be in Us**; that the world may believe that Thou didst sent Me. And the glory which Thou hast given Me, I have given to them; **that they may be one, just as We are one; I in them, and Thou in Me** that they may be perfected in unity...,"* John 17:17-23 (NAS). This is not our doing but rather part of God's perfect plan for those who have been born of the *spirit*. We partake of His divine nature and the infilling of the Holy Spirit in our spirit at the point of conversion here on earth. The infilling of the Holy Spirit not only guarantees our place in heaven but also the receiving of the 'new creation' body that is needed in heaven.

The purpose of this infilling of the Holy Spirit is for believers to become as He is - divine! *"...seeing that **His divine power** has granted to us everything pertaining to life and godliness, through the true knowledge of Him who called us by His own glory and excellence. For by these He has granted to us His precious and magnificent promises, in order that by them **you might become partakers of the divine nature**, having escaped the corruption that is in the world by lust,"* 2 Peter 1:3,4 (NAS).

Born-gain believers are commanded to take control of their soul-life; attitudes, desires, wants, thoughts, beliefs, behaviors, etc....and put them under the subjection of God's word and leading of the Holy Spirit. The

Book of Colossians is an excellent epistle to read, study and apply God's word to our daily walk in willfully choosing God's way over our own. In the Book of Colossians, God *admonishes us* to; walk worthy of the Lord, be fruitful in every good work, increase in the knowledge of God, knit our hearts in love towards other believers, attain to the knowledge of the mystery (Christ living in you), be rooted and establish in Him, know that you are complete in Him, not to let anyone judge you, and put to death; "fornication, uncleanness, passion evil desire, covetousness, anger, wrath, malice, blasphemy, filthy language," as well as put aside the old-man and put on the new-man.

Born-again believers are also to; *"put on a heart of compassion, kindness, humility, gentleness, and patience; bearing with one another, and forgiving each other…and beyond all these things put on love, which is the perfect bond of unity. And let the peace of Christ rule in your hearts," Colossians 3:1-13,14 (NAS).* This is what we are to do, and it is in our soul that these things first take place and are worked out in the body. It is imperative to understand (understanding is a process of the soul) that the body will never want to do the things of God and that God's Holy Spirit living in the born-again person's spirit will never prompt a believer to do things contrary to His word.

It is through our soul (consciousness-mind-heart), that we make the daily, minute by minute, decisions of what and who we will follow; the way of this world or the leading of the Holy Spirit, through the knowledge of scripture confirming our actions, thoughts and beliefs. The soul has many facets (mind, freewill, emotions, thought, desires, beliefs, etc.,) but like the spirit, it is not composed of parts as is the body. The body, however, is composed of many parts and goes through composition and decomposition until death occurs, at which point, total decomposition begins as the body decays and returns back to the earth. The body is reducible to molecules, atoms, particles and whatever other subatomic entities God called into existence when he created the physical universe and the human-race.

The body by itself is lifeless unless there is something within the body that empowers it to be animated. *"And the Lord God formed man of the dust of the ground, and breathed into his nostrils the breath of **life**."* *Genesis 2:7.* The soul is the immaterial conscious part of our being that grows through the acquisition of knowledge and experience of the world, God's word and the leading of the Holy Spirit. A body needs a soul and spirit to exist, however, a soul does not need a body to exist, but instead needs a spirit. A soul cannot exist apart from the spirit, ("For it is the **spirit** that gives **life**," John 6:63).

You cannot have a soul without the spirit and you cannot have a spirit without a soul. Angels, for example, are spiritual beings without a physical body, but they also express themselves with the joy of praise, *"Praise the Lord! Praise the Lord from the heavens; Praise Him in the heights! **Praise Him, all His angels**," Psalm 148:1,2 (NAS).* The soul will always be influenced by both earthly and heavenly things and events and is always in constant renewal through the process of experiencing life in this space-time continuum. For the born-again Christian, the soul is being renewed and sanctified through, the reading, studying and application of the word of God, the working of the Holy Spirit and the desire to be more Christ like.

The soul is the place where a person harbors his thoughts, beliefs, reasoning, memories, freewill, desires, emotions, and so forth. It is in our soul that the seeds of sin or holiness begin to sprout, sometimes willfully and sometimes unprovoked, by the world or by the Holy Spirit prompting our spirit.

The soul/mind is that part of a person that decides to believe in and trust in Christ as Lord and Savior or reject Him. The soul of a born-again believer will always be in conflict and in a struggle with the lusts of the world and the old-self and the leading of the Holy Spirit. There is no neutral ground to stand on that removes us from ourselves or the world. Either you are for Christ or against Him. This choice takes place in the soul. In the dialogue between Jesus and Nicodemus (John chapter 3), Jesus is clear in depicting the truth about the difference between the physical flesh and the immaterial spirit.

What is interesting to note is that in Jesus' dialogue with Nicodemus, Jesus did not mention anything about the soul. He did not say, 'that which is flesh is flesh, that which is soul is soul and that which is spirit is spirit.' His word, however, as stated in Hebrews 4:12, does assert that our soul and spirit *are able* to be pierced which enables the *dividing of the soul from the spirit.* One has only to look at a concordance, and look up the words; body, soul and spirit to understand the enormity of scriptures that give reference to the reality of the triune nature of man. I believe that it is essential to understand the reality of a born-again believer's triune nature if one is to understand what seems to be conflicting scriptures about the complete, absolute and irrevocable salvation one undergoes once the Holy Spirit has come into the spirit of that person at his or her conversion.

What I am saying here is that once a person truly receives Christ, that person cannot lose their salvation. If they could, that would mean they could repent and be saved, sin-repent and be saved, over-and-over again, every time a sin was committed. That would make salvation man-dependent rather than on what Jesus' fully satisfying sacrifice did for all humanity on the cross. That would also invalidate numerous scriptures where Jesus clearly stated that if a person believes on Him they have eternal life and that they will never perish, nor can anyone snatch them from His and the Father's hand! (John 10:27-30). That would also mean that the Holy Spirit would be on a continuous cycle of entering and leaving a person's spirit every time they sinned, that is not scriptural nor God's absolute power of salvation.

You will not find the process of being born-again-sinning-repenting, being born-again- sinning and repenting in the Bible. It would also mean that the Holy Spirit would have to violate His own word that states, *"In Him you also trusted, after you heard the word of truth, the gospel of your salvation; in whom also having believed, you were **sealed** **with the Holy Spirit of promise,** who is the **guarantee of our inheritance** until the redemption of the purchased possession, to the praise of His glory, Ephesians 1:13,14.* God's word is clear about the flesh-our body, it cannot enter, much less, inherit the kingdom of God. Our soul, on the other hand, is as indestructible as our spirit. Our spirit and soul by necessity must be indestructible if we are to spend eternity in a spiritual nonphysical dimension; either in heavenly bliss or in an eternal state of separation from God. Notice also that Jesus never stated, nor did He imply that a man can be born again and again and again as he treks through this life hoping he doesn't bite the bullet during a moment of weakness. That is not the gospel.

Think about this;

CAN A MAN BE UNBORN AGAIN? HOW CAN HE GO BACK INTO THE KINGDOM OF DARKNESS FROM WHERE GOD DELIVERED HIM FROM? HOW CAN A MAN SHED HIS ETERNAL SALVATION? HOW CAN A MAN OUT SMART, OUT WIT OR BE STRONGER THAN GOD? IF A MAN IS INCAPABLE OF GOING BACK INTO HIS MOTHER'S WOMB PHYSICALLY TO BE BORN AGAIN, HOW MUCH MORE IS A MAN INCAPABLE OF GOING BACK INTO THE WORLD FROM WHERE GOD REMOVED HIM FROM, TO BE UNBORN AGAIN? CAN A MAN WHO IS ABSOLUTELY INCAPABLE OF GETTING HIMSELF INTO HEAVEN ON HIS OWN POWER, GET HIMSELF OUT OF HEAVEN ON HIS OWN POWER? IS GOD SO IMPOTENT THAT HE CANNOT KEEP FOR HIMSELF THAT WHICH HE HIMSELF SAVED FOR HIMSELF?

*"My sheep hear my voice, and I know them, and they follow me. I give them eternal life, and they will never perish, and **no one will snatch them out of my hand**. My Father, who has given them to me, is greater than all, and **no one is able to snatch them out of my Father's hand**. I and the*

Father are one," John 10:27-30 (ESV). Jesus cannot make it any clearer about what He is saying in the above verses. He gives His true born-again believers, ETERNAL life and they will NEVER perish! 'Eternal' and 'never' declared by Jesus is what I call 'a done deal!" To add to the absoluteness of what He is saying, He declares that God the Father has given Him His sheep who cannot be taken out of His Father's hands as well as His own hands.

Who has the power to take something out of God's hand that God Himself put there and paid for through the shed blood and death of His Son!? Scripture explicitly uses the word 'soul' in many different contexts, but when it comes to the doctrine of salvation, it is very clear that it is the spirit that must be 'born-again' and it is the spirit that gives life, not the soul.

The soul does not give life to the spirit but rather the spirit to the soul. When God talks about the soul, the context of scripture will give the correct meaning of the word 'soul' within that scripture as well as line up with other scriptural verses in the Bible to confirm its use of the word 'soul,' within that particular passage. We can know if the author is talking about that part of the soul that refers to a person's ability to use the 'mental' faculties to freely (freewill) and intentionally; cognate, contemplate, quantify, qualify, judge, suspend judgment, make decisions, reason, meditate, write, read, interpret, create, etc....or use the 'emotional' component of the soul to express and feel the full spectrum of human emotions of; joy, happiness, elation, contentment, sorrow, sadness, depression, etc.... Since God will not reside with or in sin, a person can only receive the infilling of God's Holy Spirit into his/her spirit if their spirit is perfect and holy or 'born-again.'

We know just by our own experience that our soul will never get to the point of being perfect and holy or even become 'good' enough for God's Holy Spirit to come and reside in. God will only reside in that which is perfect, holy, righteous and sanctified. He will set up residence in a person's spirit only when that person believes in His Son, the Lord Jesus, at which point God makes and deems that person's *spirit*, perfect, righteous and holy, however, not the soul. The soul (mind, heart, consciousness, thoughts, emotions, etc....) of the newly regenerated-saved born-again believer is neither perfect, righteous or holy, but rather, begins to be transformed, begins to be sanctified, begins to be perfected or in other words, begins the process of sanctification.

The soul cannot begin the process of sanctification until the spirit is filled with the Holy Spirit, at which point the born-again believer's soul now has what is needed to begin to be sanctified through the power of God's Holy Spirit living in their *spirit*. The degree of sanctification that the person wishes to attain, is proportionate to the degree that he desires to be more Christ-like, and will also depend on that person's knowledge of God's word and the following of the Holy Spirit. A born-again believer should understand that the struggle between the desires of the flesh and the soul (the old-self), to do what is right in God's eyes will always be there and will always be a struggle. That is because the born-again believer's soul has access to both the old-creation and the new-creation.

A born-again believer fights the fight of faith to please God rather than his flesh, sometimes the spirit wins and sometimes the flesh wins. A perfect example can be seen by the Apostle Peter's sinful hypocritical actions in the Book of Galatians; *"Now when Peter had come to Antioch, I withstood him to his face, because he was to be blamed, for before certain men came from James, he would eat with the Gentiles; but when they came, he withdrew and separated himself, **fearing those who were of the circumcision.** And the rest of the Jews also **played the hypocrite with him** so that even Barnabas was carried away with their **hypocrisy.** But when I saw that they were **not straight forward about the truth of the gospel,** I said to Peter before them all, "If you, being a Jew, live in the manner of Gentiles and not as the Jews, why do you compel Gentiles to live as Jews?" Galatians 2:11-14.* In this passage of scripture, the great Apostle Paul is rebuking the great Apostle Peter for his hypocritical behavior and untruthful portrayal of the gospel in front of the Gentiles. The Apostle Peter was fearful of the Jew's who continued to believe that one must follow the Law (the Old Testament Laws prescribe to the nation of Israel) to rightfully follow God. He was fearful of the negative rejection or judgment about him from these certain men.

The Apostle Paul goes on to explain the reality of the gospel of Christ to Peter; *"We who are Jews by nature, and not sinners of the Gentiles, knowing that a man is **not justified by the works of the law** but **by faith in Jesus Christ,** even we have believed in Christ Jesus, that we might be **justified by faith in Christ** and **not** by the **works of the law;** for by the works of the law **no flesh shall be justified,"** Galatians 2:15,16.* It is because of God's mercy through the sacrifice of Christ on the cross that the unperfected state of a person's soul and its intertwined relationship with the world, Satan's power and their own personal sinful unregenerate body, and their 'in the process of sanctification' soul that there will *never be any condemnation from God* towards the born-again believer who struggles through this conflict.

'Believing' in Christ gets us *into* heaven and sanctifying our soul not only causes us to grow in the knowledge of Christ, but also to grow in grace and total forgiveness even though we sin while struggling not to sin. Every time we choose to not sin, but instead follow the desires of God, we not only grow spiritually, but God also counts our effort towards heavenly rewards! Brother's and Sister's in Christ, God is a rewarder and when He rewards you, you will receive rewards that are incomprehensible to the human mind and can only be appreciated and enjoyed while you are in your indestructible, new-creation, heavenly body within the spirit realm.

God does reward us while we are here on earth, but the heavenly rewards are eternal and not temporal as is this world. The Apostle Paul was fully aware of the war that waged between his own sinful body, soul and his spirit. *"For that which I am doing, I do not understand; for I am not practicing what I would like to do, but **I am doing the very thing I hate**. But if I do the very thing I do not wish to do, I agree with the Law, confessing that it is good. So now, **no longer am I the one doing it, but sin which indwells me**,"* Romans 7:15-18 (NAS). *"There is therefore, **no more condemnation for those who are in Christ Jesus**,"* Romans 8:1 (NAS).

'Doing' refers to the *body* and 'understanding' refers to the *soul*, while 'I' refers to the Apostle Paul's *spirit*. At this point I am going to take some leeway in trying to get across the reality of the removal of condemnation from the sinful thoughts and actions of born-again believers. I will restate Romans 7:15-18 with a twist, to try to make clear, my point; *"For that which the Apostle Paul is doing, he does not understand; for the Apostle Paul is not practicing what he would like to do, but he is doing the very thing he hates. But if the Apostle Paul does the very thing he wishes not to do, he agrees with the Law, confessing that it is good. So now, no longer is the Apostle Paul the one doing it, but sin which indwells him"!*

It is imperative that we understand that a born-again believer is not justified by the law, but rather by believing in Christ Jesus. It is also the spirit that is justified, perfect and holy. As we can see both the Apostle Peter and Paul struggle within their body and soul to do what is right. That is because they lived in a physical body that wanted what the physical body wanted along with what the old-man or the old-self (in the soul/ mind) wanted. We also live in a physical fleshly body, that will never stop wanting what it wants when it wants it-it is unredeemable, "the flesh counts for nothing!" We also possess, as they possessed, a soul that contains the knowledge and awareness of the new-self along with the old-self.

Our soul fights within itself to choose what the old-man wants or what the new-man wants. The Bible does not hold any punches, it clearly depicts the great men of God doing what it is we do today, sin in word, thought and deed. However, the good news is that Christ Jesus died for ALL our sins! Our spirit does not need to follow or keep the law, first, because we are incapable of doing such a feat, and second, Jesus already followed and completed every requirement of the law. Since He lives in our spirit, the completion of the law is already within our spirit and not in our soul. It is within our spirit that the Spirit of God lives, it is in our soul that we have the old-man and the ever growing new-man residing.

We must choose, daily, and sometimes on a minute by minute basis, to follow Christ (what the new-man wants) or follow the world (what the old-man wants). The more we follow Christ the more we grow in His grace, and even though we try to live a Godly life, we will at times miss the mark. As we can see in scripture, great men of God were also in desperate need of God's grace and mercy for them to walk worthy of the Lord, without condemnation.

God's mercy and grace are ever present at the time of conversion and therefore, there was never any condemnation for them and neither is there any condemnation for us today. Think about this for a moment; "no more condemnation for those who are in Christ Jesus," "no more condemnation for those who are in Christ Jesus," "no more condemnation for those who are in Christ Jesus!" Let that sink into your spirit. I know that we can read it and understand its meaning in our mind, however, this message must move out of our intellectual understanding and anchor into our spirit-the real you!

*"But when the goodness and loving kindness of God our Savior appeared, He saved us, not because of works done by us in **righteousness** but **according to His own mercy**," Titus 3:4-5. Look at this passage again, "not because of works done in **righteousness**..."* The word used here is 'righteousness' not **un**righteousness. This means that not even good righteous works will save a person on judgment day, only through the

merciful shed blood of Christ is anyone able to get saved. God's removal of the penalty and power of sin through the shedding of Christ's blood and His death on the cross for the sins of the world, frees us from all condemnation when we sin ignorantly as well as purposefully, as we struggle to be free from sin and its consequences.

It is this struggle that the soul has with the flesh that many Christians judge other Christians of not being true Christians, not realizing that they themselves are being un-Christ like in their judgment of other brothers and sisters in Christ. This is usually done out of a self-righteous indignant spirit rather than out of a spirit of love and concern for the spiritual well-being of the Christian in question. Love for the brethren is peaceable and easy to see, however, condemnation bears down on the soul of both.

As stated above, there are many facets and complex intricacies to our soul, and our mind is, without a doubt, one of them. It is of utmost importance to gain some understanding of our mind, the purpose of our mind and the author of our mind. *"do not be conformed to this world, but be transformed by the **renewing of your mind**, that you may prove what is that good and acceptable and perfect will of God,"* Romans 12:2. *"Set your **mind** on things above, not on things on earth,"* Colossians 3:2. What is clear in these scriptures is that it is God's will that we be renewed in our 'mind.' We know that the mind resides within the soul, and is always in need of being renewed, that it may come in line with our newly created spirit. This is not as complicated a concept as one might think, for example, we understand the concept of buying a young child a pair of expensive shoes just slightly larger than what they are for the purpose of the child growing into their shoes, or the idea of being promoted at work into a position that one has one never occupied, but is told that they will learn everything needed to perform their job as time allows them to work up to the jobs requirements, the Presidency of the United States is a great example.

No one becomes the President of the United States by first having to have the experience of being the President of the United States!? Once a person wins the presidency, is inaugurated and sworn in, they are now officially the President of the United States and during their first day in the Oval Office that person begins to learn to act, behave and perform the duties as the President of the United States. In the same manner when one is born-again they have been deemed 'a child of God,' *"Behold what manner of love the Father has bestowed on us, that **we should be called children of God**," 1 John 3:1,* and must learn to *transform their mind* that they may *learn* to act as a 'children of God.'

You know you have a mind, however, you are not our mind! This may sound a bit strange, however, if you think about this, **you** make up **your** mind to do, or not do something, hundreds of times per day. When you declare; "my mind is made up," you don't really mean that your mind made an executive decision without your consent or that you are without any control over what your mind may or may not do without your approval. Any rational, sane person knows whether he or she is in charge of their mind. If you're able to change, set, or manipulate something at your choosing, the thing you manipulated cannot be you. For example, when you use your mind to think of a thought, you do not become the thought, rather you are on the outside of the thought thinking about that thought, sometimes judging if that thought is valid, funny, decent, indecent, etc., *"For I delight in the law of God according to the inward man. But I see another law in my members, warring against the law of **my mind,** and bringing me into captivity to the law of sin which is in my members,...So then, **with the mind I myself serve the law of God,** but with the flesh the law of sin,"* Romans 7:22,23,25.

It seems evident that the Apostle Paul will use the 'I' part of himself (the inward man, or his spirit), to engage his mind (his soul) to serve God, *"So then, with the mind"* (soul), *I* (spirit) *myself serve the law of God,"* but with his flesh (his body), he will use to serve the law of sin, *"but with the flesh the law of sin,"* that is, only when he does sin. When God puts His laws (not the commandments given to Israel, but the Laws of Christ; to love the Lord God with all your mind, heart-soul and to love others as yourself!), into the mind of the born-again believer, it is for the believer to have the spiritual capabilities to learn all they can about serving the one and only true God.

It is also clear that it is us that must do the *renewing of our mind.* When we renew our mind, through the reading of God's word and leading of the Holy Spirit, it is our soul, our mind, our consciousness that begins to experience the goodness of the Lord. It is our soul that begins to acquire peace, it is our soul that cries out Abba Father! We must do the work of sanctifying our soul, and we do this, every time we say 'yes'! to God and 'no!' to the world. If our soul was *born-again* at the point of conversion, we would not need to *renew* it. God's word, however, tells us to renew our mind, but never tells us to renew our spirit, for only He can do that!

CHAPTER 6

THE SPIRIT

"IT IS THE SPIRIT THAT GIVES LIFE," John 6:63

What animates the body and the soul is life. Another word for life is 'spirit.' The body, soul and spirit can be conceptualized as a bottle of water. The bottle is the body (flesh), hydrogen is the soul (heart, mind, consciousness, freewill, etc....) and oxygen is the spirit (life, aliveness). Hydrogen and Oxygen are what water is comprised of and both are necessary for water to exist. Water will only be contained by the confines and boundaries it is surrounded by. In the same manner, a person is soul and spirit within the confines and boundaries of a physical body, which is only the carrier of the soul and spirit *in this physical universe.*

The bottle, being like the body, will end up in a landfill or in other words, in the grave. It can never become something different than what it is-human. The body will always be physical, made up of particles, atoms, molecules, and cells. The immaterial soul, being immaterial like the spirit, can never achieve perfection in this world.

If you study the life of the great apostles in the New Testament you will quickly see that even after these men had lived with Jesus and did mighty miracles when they were with Him, still sinned in words, thoughts and deeds. They struggled daily with their own sin as do all born-again believers today. We can, as they did, move our soul/mind/ consciousness towards perfection, sanctification and holiness, but only after the conversion of the spirit,

"Truly, truly, I say to you, unless one is **born again** *he cannot see the kingdom of God," "Truly, truly, I say to you, unless one is born of water* **and the Spirit***, he cannot enter the kingdom of God," John 3:3, 5 (ESV), "The kingdom of heaven does not come with observation; nor will they say, 'See here! or 'See there!' For indeed,* **the kingdom of God is within you,"** *Luke 17:20.*

Without the Holy Spirit of God inside your spirit, the soul and the spirit are lost! The soul of an unbeliever will always be at odds with the things of God because he/she does not have the Spirit of God living in their spirit, thus the unbeliever's soul is lost along with their dead-to-God spirit. The soul, however, of a born-again believer, can engage in acts of God through the leading of the Holy Spirit and through a self-conscious freewill willingness to do so. He can also freely choose not to act on the leading of the Holy Spirit. That is, God will not force someone to act on His behalf, but rather, He will use a willing heart. Without the Holy Spirit of God living inside a person's spirit, there is no born-again conversion and thus nothing spiritual or heavenly within that person's spirit that would allow that person to even think about the one and only true God, much less engage in the righteous acts of God.

The spirit of a born-again believer is filled with the *fullness* of God's Holy Spirit, *"God* ***does not give*** *the Spirit by* ***measure," John 3:34.* When God breathed life (spirit) into the physical lifeless body of Adam, he immediately became, not only animated, but also conscious of his own consciousness. Adam was able to reason, contemplate, create, etc. in what every human mind engages in throughout their lives. God's purpose for you started with God's full knowledge that Adam and Eve would fall in the Garden of Eden.

The fall was part of His all-knowing and perfect plan for the entire human race. The plan of God is for us to live within this physical realm in a physical body with a soul that has that ability to reason, contemplate and make freewill decisions between choosing the things of this world or the things of God while living in this world. Without the spirit of God living within our spirit this is an impossibility. If we freely choose Him, He will put His Spirit into our *spirit*, and will let us partake of His divine *spiritual* nature when we exit this world, so we can live in His immaterial heavenly spiritual realm for all eternity. Remember, one hundred years of life on this earth is insignificant when compared to eternity. This is the choice we must make while we are alive here on earth.

What makes understanding the things of the spirit difficult is the fact that we cannot feel our spirit as we can feel our body and soul. This causes many people to become disjunctive in their reasoning when they try to ascribe to the soul what only belongs to the spirit. Biblically speaking, we are to use the components of our soul (thoughts/mind/reasoning) to decide by faith (in our soul) to believe God and what His word says about what our spiritual condition is in, regardless of how we feel. What is needed for any born-again believer to grow spiritually, is for the born-again believer to put his emotions, thoughts and bodily sensations under the subjection of God, if he/she is to learn the absolute truths about all of life, whether about this physical world or the invisible heavenly realms.

Our *soul* and *fleshly body* cannot and will never be transformed in to a new creation through the born-again experience, *"That which is born of flesh is flesh, and that which is **born of the Spirit is <u>spirit</u>,**" John 3:6. (ESV). "It is the <u>**Spirit**</u> who gives life; the flesh profits nothing, "John 6:63.* The soul can, however, be greatly influence by the things of God, *"The law of the Lord is perfect, converting the soul," Psalms 19:7.* None of the Old Testament saints were ever *born-again* or transformed into a *new creation.* The reason is because Jesus had not been born, and his sacrifice for the sins of the world had not been actualized. Both the spirit and the soul are immaterial and intertwined so that one will not exist without the other.

When a person is 'lost' or not 'saved, both his soul and spirit are lost. Being 'lost' in the Biblical sense means that God is not your heavenly Father, and therefore, you cannot have a personal relationship with Him through Jesus Christ. Second, a nonbeliever, who does not have the Holy Spirit living in their *spirit,* is what 'lost' or 'losing your life' (spirit) means, remember that your spirit and soul, although they are separated by God for His purposes, will always be intertwined. *"For what shall a man be profited, if he gains the whole world, and forfeit his **life**? or what shall a man give in exchange for his **life**?" (ASV), "For whoever would save his life will lose it, but whoever loses his life for my sake will find it. For what will it profit a man if he gains the whole world and forfeits his **soul**? Or what shall a man give in return for his **soul**?" Matthew 16:25,26 (ESV).*

The soul, although not sanctified or made holy, is always connected to the spirit. A person's spirit is the only part of their triune nature that can be regenerated, or in other words, born-again, made and deemed perfect, holy and sanctified by God. The separation of soul and spirit, as stated in Hebrews 4:12, is likened to a person separating his thoughts from his emotions in that they are both immaterial and taking place within the nonphysical realm, but nevertheless, they will always be united. How God separates the soul from the spirit is a spiritual event or process we will never understand while we live in this physical universe. This separation of the spirit from the soul is not only necessary, but also apparent to any born-again believer who *knows,* without a doubt, the condition of their soul/mind/conscience and its bent towards thinking, feeling and acting sinful and totally against God's will. *"For I do not do the good I want, but he evil I do not want is what I keep on doing. Now if I do what I do not want, it is no longer I who do it, but sin that dwells within me," Romans 7:19,20 (ESV).*

There are a multitude of scriptures that clearly define the condition of our sinful nature that lies within our flesh and in our soul. *"If we say we have no sin, we **deceive ourselves**, and the truth is not in us," 1 John 1:8.* Deception is not of the flesh, but rather, the immaterial mind/soul. Once again, although we can feel our soul and know our thoughts as well as feel our body, we cannot feel our spirit. It is **by faith** that we know we are saved by the sacrifice of Christ.

I feel that at this point in the book I should share my 'born-again' experience in hopes of clarifying any confusion that may be presented in this chapter. I would like to start out by saying that in no way am I trying to glamorize godless living. I will simply state the facts of what I, as a nonbeliever, experienced before, during and after my born-again conversion.

Prior to receiving Jesus, I had been a professional guitar player traveling world-wide. My life was all about drugs, sex and rock and roll. After getting out of the band, I got married and had two children, and continued using drugs. I also had grown up Catholic and I had always believed in God. I even tried reading the Bible, but it made no sense to me. One afternoon while giving guitar lessons, I was about to ask one of my students, who happen to look like a pot smoking hippie, if he, by any chance, had any 'weed' on him (I had never asked a student for this kind of favor, but I was getting desperate!). The student turned out to be an Associate Pastor of a church! Just as I was about to ask him, he looked me in the eye and asked, "would you be interested in a Bible study?"

The first thought that came to my mind was, "oh my God, a Jesus freak! Whew! that was a close one, good thing I didn't ask him." Then I thought about it for a while and the reality was that I had already been searching. I had taken the time to talk with Jehovah Witnesses when they came to my home and I even tried being a Buddhist when I was stationed in Iwakkuni, Japan, while serving in the Marine Corps. So, I told him, yes! I would be interested in having a Bible study.

That evening, my guitar student and his wife came to my home, and by the nights end, I had received Jesus as my Lord and Savior. That weekend I also got baptized at the church. The baptism was a great point of contention for me. I was surrounded by people who were telling me that I was going to feel fantastic and that I was going to be a 'new creation,' when I came up out of the water, a new person! As they pulled me up out of the water everyone was singing and praising God, but not me! I thought to myself, "there is no God!' All this time throughout my life, I have been believing a sham." I felt horrible, betrayed and greatly disappointed. I played the part and smiled as if something great had happened to me.

But the reality was that I felt empty inside. I wanted to scream and cry at the same time. How could this happen to me. I was an Altar Boy growing up and served at church, I knew without a doubt that there was a God, however, knowing that I felt no different coming up out of the water just hammered away in my mind. I started to have a great conflict within my mind and within my soul. Over and over in my mind I kept saying; There is a God...no there is not, no, there must be a God, there cannot not be a God...no, there is no God. I tried to figure out why I did not FEEL the way I was told I was going to feel. I cried and struggled with this conflict. The greatest point of anguish was when I concluded that there was a God, and the problem was not that God did not exist, but rather the problem was with me, not God.

I was not good enough, I had been rejected by God! That was the only logical conclusion I could come to, and I did. I cried for a week. There were no words to express my anguish during that week. The good news, obviously, is that something happened to me that changed my mind and cleared the way to the truth of my situation; God's word! *"Be transformed by the renewing of your mind,"* Romans 12:2. This is a most appropriate place for this scripture. What happened to me was that my wife, stated to me; "don't you know what is happening to you? You're being attacked by the devil, that's what happened to Jesus after he got baptized." I thought about what she said for a moment and realized that that made sense. I then started all over with the; yes, I'm saved, no I'm not, yes I am,...over and over again! The point of change took place when I *made a decision -* the greatest decision of my life! I said to myself; "I'm saved, and that's all there is to it. God is real, He exists, and He saved me, period, I don't care how I FEEL, I am saved!

That is when my life really changed. The veil was lifted from my mind. I began not only immersing myself in scripture, but also understanding it! I've written here about my conversion, that took place thirty years ago, to say that hindsight is 20/20. I now understand the reality of my *spirit* being born of God's Holy Spirit and the reality of the struggle within my soul, daily, in an ever-aging body. I can most definitely feel my body and my soul, however, there is no feeling to my spirit, but there is God's truth that feeds my spirit through the reading, studying and most important, the application of His word to my life. You can gage spiritual growth by the changes that take place in your soul/mind; reasoning, freewill, desires, etc.... as well as in the things you do with your body.

It is God's Holy Spirit living in the believer's spirit that allows the believer to use their soul to give thanks for their salvation. It is in our body that we glorify God by the things we do or don't do for His purposes. As every true born-again believer knows, the good news is; *"If we walk in the light, as He is in the light, we have fellowship with one another, and the* blood of Jesus His Son cleanses us from **all** sin," 1 John 1:7 (ESV), or in other words, if you receive Jesus Christ as Lord and savior, you are saved, born-again and regenerated by the infilling of the Holy Spirit who comes to live in you.

At this point of regeneration, every sin that you have ever committed, are committing, and will commit, are completely and totally forgiven! "Blessed are those whose lawless deeds **are forgiven** (past sins!), and whose sins **are covered** (present sins!); Blessed is the man to whom the Lord **shall not impute** sin (future!)," Romans 4:7,8. "He has appeared **once for all** at the end of the ages to **put away sin** by the sacrifice of Himself," Hebrews 9:26 (ESV). It is a one-time event. God will not divorce you, abandon you or leave you - ever, just because you sinned. "I will never leave you or forsake you," "I am with you always, even to the end of the age," Hebrews 13:5, and Matthew 28:20. "My sheep hear my voice, and I know them, and they follow Me. And I give them **eternal life**, and they shall **never perish;** neither shall anyone snatch them out of My hand. My Father, who has given them to Me, is greater than all; and **no one is able to snatch them out of my Father's hand.** I and My Father are one," John 14:27-30.

The scriptures are clear about a Spirit filled born-again believer's sins and what God, through Jesus, has done for their sins, not only of the believer, but also the sins of the world, however, when we add; "Whoever has been born of God **does not sin**, for His seed remains in him; and **he cannot sin,** because he has been born of God," 1 John 3:9. "We know that whoever is born of God **does not sin,** 1 John 5:18, it's easy to see how confusion can rear its ugly head, especially when we are explicitly and experientially aware of our sinful thoughts, words and deeds that we experience daily.

After reading God's word, that states in a nutshell, that every 'born-again' believer; does *not* and *cannot* sin, confusion and doubt emerge along with many other negative thoughts and feelings. It is a serious violation of, not only God's word, but also of the sacrifice of Christ Jesus, and what He had to endure to remove, cleanse, and forgive us, of all our sins, when one thinks that he must live a perfect sinless or almost sinless life in order to be acceptable to God, in hopes of making it into His heavenly kingdom.

So then, how do we reconcile the following facts; 1.) You have received Christ Jesus as Lord and Savior and you know that you are a true born-again believer, 2.) You know that you sin in word, thought and deed, and 3.) God's word clearly states that those who have been born of God, *do not* and *cannot* sin?

If you believe that you do not sin, then, as stated in 1 John 1:8; *"If we say we have no sin, we **deceive** ourselves, and the truth is not in us,"* you are deluded, you're deceiving yourself, a sure sign of not being a true born-again believer. However, if you agree that you do sin, then this does not sit well with, 1 John 3:9 stated above; *"Whoever has been born of God **does not sin**, for His seed remains in him; and **he cannot sin,** because he has been born of God."* The reality is that many people turn their back on God, and reject God's word, due to what they may see as inconsistencies or contradictions that they find in the Bible.

Let me be very clear at this point, there is no contradiction. *"It is the spirit that gives life, the flesh profits nothing,"* John 6:63. *"unless one is born again, he cannot see the kingdom of God,"* John 3: 3. Once again; the flesh or the body cannot be, and will never be sanctified, justified or regenerated. The soul although it is attached to the believer's spirit *begins the process* of sanctification through the leading of the Holy Spirit, which is now housed within the spirit of the born-again believer. The soul is always in constant confrontation with the world, demonic forces and the old self, that is why every true born-again believer knows that they sin.

The *spirit* of a born-again believer is filled with God's Holy Spirit and is always perfect, and sanctified, *"For by one offering He hath **perfected forever** them that **are sanctified,** Hebrews 10:14 (ASV).* The spirit of a born-again believer is the Holy of Holies (God's Holy Temple) where God's Holy Spirit resides and where one becomes one with God the Father, His Spirit and with His Son, Jesus. *"Do you not know that you are the temple of God and that the Spirit of God **dwells in you,**"* 1 Corinthians 3:16. This is the 'mystery' that the Bible talks about, the mystery is 'Christ in us,' *"for the sake of His body, which is the church, of which I became a minister according to the stewardship from God which was given to me for you, to fulfill the word of God, **the mystery** which has been hidden from ages and from generations, but **has now been revealed** to His saints. To them God willed to make known what are the riches of the glory, of **this mystery** among the Gentiles: which is **Christ in you**, the hope of glory,"* Colossians 1:24-27.

There is no sin in a born-again believer's spirit because God the Father has deemed that person's spirit to be sanctified, holy and perfect due to their **belief in Christ** and His shed blood and sacrifice for the sins of the world! *"For by one offering, He **has perfected forever** those who are **being sanctified**, Hebrews 10:14.* This sounds counterintuitive because we *know* ourselves. Me perfect! I don't think so. If Christ Jesus were living in our bodies, are bodies would never die, if Christ Jesus were living in our soul, we would never sin! God, however, has chosen the act of 'believing,' to be the manner, in which one can attain perfection in their *spirit* and receive eternal life, now,! while we live in this physical realm.

This 'believing' must be and can only be in Christ Jesus as the Savior of the world! *"In Him you also trusted, after you heard the word of truth, the gospel of your salvation; in whom also having **believed,** you were **sealed with the Holy Spirit** of promise, who is the guarantee of our inheritance until the redemption of the purchased possession, to the praise of His glory," Ephesians 1:13,14.* Believing is a function of the soul and is intertwined with a person's freewill/consciousness.

Once a person, using their freewill 'believes' on the Lord Jesus Christ, their **spirit** is 'born-again,' *"Most assuredly, I say to you, unless on is born again, he cannot see the kingdom of God." "Most assuredly, I say to you, unless one is born of water **and the Spirit,** he cannot enter the kingdom of God. "That which is born of the flesh is flesh, and that which is born of the Spirit **is spirit**. "Do not marvel that I said to you, 'You must be born again,' The wind blows where it wishes, and you cannot tell where it* *comes from and where it goes. So is everyone who is **born of the Spirit**,"* *John 3:3,5-8.*

The born-again event takes place in the heart of the believer and culminates with the infilling of God's Holy Spirit into our spirit. That is 'the mystery of God,' - Christ in you! The Holy Spirit of God, God Himself, living inside your spirit! You can love the Lord God with all your heart, soul and mind, but you cannot love Him unless your spirit is born-again! *"But the hour cometh, and now is, when the true worshippers shall worship the Father in **spirit and truth**: for such doth the Father seek to be His worshippers. God is a Spirit: and they that worship Him must worship in spirit and truth," John 4:23,24 (ASV).*

God, in His word talks about humanity in the past, present and future tense, as well as within the physical earthly and eternal, non-physical spiritual heavenly realms while they both are occurring consecutively and simultaneously! This is because He exists outside of time. What we were prior to conversion, what we are now after our conversion in; body, soul and spirit, what we are now in the spiritual realm, while we are here on earth, and at the same time, where we are and who we are in the spiritual realm and in the age to come, is known by God, for He knows all there is that can be known about you; past, present and future, here and there now, and in the future.

A serious point must be made here. God wishes that no one spend eternity in hell, however, since God is a loving and just God, He will not force someone to love Him, and loving Him is what being born-again is all about. We loved Him, because He first loved us. When we come to the realization of the love of God through the birth, life, death, and resurrection of Christ Jesus, then we have come to the 'valley of decision.' Will we accept Him or reject Him? God will chase us until we are buried in the ground. At every turning point in our life God is chasing us, He wishes no one to be lost. On Judgment Day, no one will be able to point the finger at God and blame Him for where they are going to spend eternity. *"For what man knows the thoughts of the man except the spirit of the man which is in him?" 1 Corinthians 2:11.*

Notice that in the above passage, thoughts and spirit are two totally different things. Thoughts are not who you are, but rather they are what you (spirit) desire to think about. They are the workings of your creative spirit that are conjured up in your mind/soul and expressed through your physical body (lungs, vocal cords, etc.,). Your spirit is who you really are, and you are the only one aside from God who knows your thoughts. That is why you (spirit) can create, contemplate and even change your thoughts and mind continually and daily throughout your life while you continue to be you!

You and only you, religious or nonreligious, can decide to live with God for all eternity or live, for all eternity without Him. No amount of earthly religious or non-religious counseling, Bible thumping or hell and damnation preaching can cause the spirit to want to be 'born-again,' much less actually be 'born-again.' Only God's wooing through the presence and power of the Holy Spirit, can a person come to God the Father through His Son, Jesus Christ, and only through the drawing in of God the Father towards His Son can we be drawn to Christ. *"No one can come to Me unless the Father draws him to me…." "For by grace you have been saved through faith, and that not of yourselves it is the* **gift of God**, **not of works,** *lest anyone should boast. For* **we** *are* **HIS** *workmanship, created in Christ Jesus for good works, which* **GOD** *prepared before-hand that* **we should** **walk in them**," *Ephesians 2:8-10.*

At this point I think it is important to understand that Jesus (God incarnate) draws ALL men to Himself, *"And as Moses lifted up the serpent in the wilderness, so must the Son of Man be lifted up, that* **whoever** **believes** *in Him may have eternal life," "And I, when I am lifted up from the earth,* **will draw all people** *to* **Myself**." *John 3:14, 12:32 (ESV).* Everyone is drawn to Jesus, either to worship Him or blaspheme Him, there is no neutral or middle ground. Even those who could care less about Jesus, and who have no thought about his existence or non-existence, blaspheme against Jesus in that rejecting Christ is itself a blasphemy.

The significance of the sacrifice of Jesus is an event that is beyond human comprehension. Christ Jesus himself clearly and simply stated that 'whoever' *believes* in Him *has* eternal life, it is as simple as that. Eternal life is granted, at the point of conversion, while we are alive here on earth. Being 'lifted up' is an expression of His suffering and sacrifice when He was 'lifted up' on the cross. He clearly stated numerous times that, "whoever believes," has eternal life. He also made it clear that when He would be 'lifted up,' He would draw *all* people to Himself. Jesus does not ask a person to understand the full gravity of his mission prior to receiving Him as Lord and Savior, but rather, just believe that He is who He says He is.

Once a person believes on the Lord Jesus, God deems that person's *spirit* perfect, sanctified and holy. To God, that person is alive to Him and born-again through the infilling of the Holy Spirit. Both the spirit and soul are now free from the penalty and power of sin, because, it is the '*spirit,*' that is now perfect, now holy and now sanctified and cannot NOT be perfect, holy and sanctified, for God will only reside in what is perfect, holy and sanctified.

The spirit and soul of a born-again believer has been redeemed or, in other words, bought back by God to Himself through the shed blood, death and resurrection of Jesus. At the point of conversion, there is no miraculous instantaneous change of the soul, as there is for the 'spirit.'

At the point of conversion, a person's spirit is immediately, *"delivered from the power of darkness and conveyed us into the kingdom of the Son of His love, in whom we have redemption through His blood, the forgiveness of sins,"* Colossians 1:13,14. This is the reality for any true born-again believer; 'delivered' and 'conveyed' are in the past-tense form. It is a completed task!

The problem many Christians struggle with is the lack of understanding of the difference between the spirit and the soul. When a person gets saved their personality, knowledge, worldview, reasoning, etc....will now have to, by faith, draw on the leading of the Holy Spirit and the reading and study of the scriptures, if they want to be Christ like in all areas of their life.

The indestructible, born-again, 'God filled *spirit*' is complete, while the *soul,* prior to being born-again, intertwined with the spirit and now separated from the spirit, is in constant need of being renewed. God has left that up for us to accomplish, we do the renewing of our soul/personality/reasoning, etc. There is much stated in the Bible (New Testament) about what we as 'born-again in the spirit' believers are to engage our souls in, such as; *renewing our minds, walking by faith, loving the brethren, forgiving one another, stealing no more, no longer engaging in; fornication, adultery, or other sexual perversions,* but instead, now; *engaging in good works prepared by God, helping those in need, living a holy life, etc.*

If a person receives Jesus Christ as Lord and Savior at the age of twenty-five, then that person has twenty-five years of faulty, incorrect and skewed thinking, believing and reasoning. The personality, reasoning, thoughts and feelings (soul) must come in line with God's word, however, the spirit, at the point of conversion, is already complete and lacks nothing because the creator of all creation, the omnipotent, omniscient God is living within their spirit! Once created, a person's spirit is indestructible, as is their soul. It is the spirit that is 'alive' and it is the soul that expresses the 'aliveness.' It is the spirit and soul that will experience the bliss of heaven or the torment of hell. Every conscious person (soul) will experience the eternal place they choose to reside in for all eternity.

If a person believes in Jesus Christ, as the scriptures implores us to do, one of the rewards they will experience is eternal life in heaven with their creator. I say, 'one of the rewards,' because God wants to give us many rewards for our service for Him while we are alive on earth. *"Do you not know that you are the temple of God and that the **Spirit of God dwells in you?**" 1 Corinthians 3:16.* Once again, Yes, God dwells in the very spirit of every 'born-again' believer. God *in you* (if you are a born-again believer) is a reality that has already been actualized in every born-again believer's *spirit* and is longed for by the soul.

We long to be with our heavenly Father because we now know, or we should know that the creator of all that exist in this universe and in the spiritual heavenly realms is our FATHER! And He is living inside our spirit! This is the 'mystery' that scripture alludes to when talking about the 'new creation.' The mystery that has now been revealed to us in our spirit.

Now that the Holy Spirit lives in our spirit, we can now begin the process, through the spirit, of not only sanctifying our soul, but acquiring spiritual understanding of God's truth in scripture as well as becoming attuned to the leading of the Holy Spirit, *"But as it is written; "Eye has not seen, nor ear heard, nor have entered into the heart of man, the things which God has prepared for those who love Him.* **But God has revealed them to us** *through His spirit*, 1 Corinthians 2:9,10.

Jesus Christ has completed His mission here on earth but continues to perform His duty as our High Priest sitting at the right hand of God the Father acting as an advocate for every born-again believer, *"My little children, these things I write to you, so that you may not sin. And if anyone sins, we have an Advocate with the Father, Jesus Christ the righteous,"* 1 John 2:1.

CHAPTER 7

THE CONFLICT

"For what I am doing, I do not understand. For what I will to do, that I do not practice; but what I hate, that I do," Romans 7:15.

This 'conflict' in chapter 7 of the Book of Romans is one of the most known realities that a true 'born-again' believer, experiences. If I am a new creation in Christ Jesus and Christ is living in me and I want to live a righteous life for God, why do I still sin in word, thought and/or deed? And why do I feel so guilty and horrible when I do sin? Am I really saved? Will I ever stop sinning? These are but a few questions that both new converts and long-time believers struggle with.

This struggle is one that the apostle Paul was obviously quite familiar with and which is easily observed in the 7th chapter of Romans verses 14 through 24. *"For we know that the law is spiritual, but I am of the flesh, sold under sin. For I do not understand my own actions. For I do not do what I want, but I do the very thing I hate. Now if I do what I do not want, I agree with the law, that it is good. So now it is no longer I who do it, but sin that dwells within me. For I know that nothing good dwells within me, that is in my flesh. For I have the desire to do what is right, but not the ability to carry it out. For I do not do the good I want, but he evil I do not want is what I keep on doing. Now if I do what I do not want, it is no longer I who do it, but sin that dwells within me. So, I find it to be a law that when I want to do right, evil lies close at hand. For I delight in the law of God, in my inner being, but I see in my members another law waging war against the law of my mind and making me captive to the law of sin that dwells in my members. Wretched man that I am! Who will deliver me from this body of death?" Romans 7:14-24 (ESV).* Dear brothers and sisters in Christ, only a true born-again believer could write this passage. Only true born-again believers go through this type of struggle. Only true born-again believers are conscious of their sinful thoughts, words and deeds and the inclination they continue to have towards *ungodliness.* The battle that is waged against our spirit by our own body, mind, the world, Satan and his demonic forces, is the battle that all true born-again believers are confronted with. If you struggle with this kind of conflict, then your struggle is a sure sign that you are 'born-again'.

True born-again believers never had this conflict until they were 'born-again'! It is through this struggle and through the leading of the Holy Spirit that we mature as true born-again believers as we increase in the knowledge of Christ through the reading and application of His word.

A babe in Christ may give up their walk with the Lord simply because he cannot understand or reconcile what seem to be apparent contradictions in the Bible, however a 'babe in Christ' will not lose their salvation, but rather, will lose rewards that God is eager to given him for his faithfulness and accomplishments of the good works He has prepared for him walk into, *"For we are his workmanship, created in Christ Jesus for good works, which God prepared beforehand, that we should walk in them, Ephesians 2:10.*

How is it that the Bible tells us not to sin (and we know that we do sin daily), and that the person who does sin will be condemned to eternal damnation in one scripture and yet in another scripture we are told that we are perfect, sanctified and that we cannot sin, *"Whoever has been born of God does not sin, because he has been born of God," 1 John 3:8,9.* There is no contradiction here. Born-again believers are told not to sin, however, the Bible also states that if we do sin, we have an advocate before God the Father, who stands in our place, Jesus Christ! *"My little children, these things I write to you, so that you may not sin. And **if anyone sins, we have an Advocate with the Father, Jesus Christ** the righteous. And He himself is the propitiation for our sins, and not for ours only but also for the whole world," 1 John 2:1,2.*

Jesus advocates for the sins done in the body and soul of the believer. The spirit of the believer is 'born-again' and cannot sin. We know, however, that when we do sin we feel guilty, shameful, condemned, etc....This should not be the case, for Christ Jesus has paid the penalty for sin as well has rendered powerless the effects of sin through the sacrifice of Himself, *"but now, once at the end of the ages, He has appeared to **put away sin** by the sacrifice of Himself," Hebrews 9:26, "**Their sins and lawless deeds I will remember no more**. Now where there is **remission of these,** there is no longer an offering for sin," Hebrews 10:17,18.* Am I saying that as believer's we can just go out and sin as much as we desire because God does not hold our sin against us? Absolutely not! If you are truly born-again, then you, as a believer, will want to do what is right in God's sight, but you will also find it hard to overcome past sinful habits without calling on God to help you. God is wanting His children to call on Him in times of need as well as in times of want.

Let us examine Roman's 7:14-24 line by line, precept by precept using God's word as well as the reasoning abilities God has infused into our minds, *"come let us reason together," Isaiah 1:18,* that we may come to the full understanding God intends for us to understand concerning sin.

For we know that the law is spiritual; The law that the Apostle Paul is talking about is specific to spiritual matters. Paul is making a declaration to those who know about spiritual matters as well as matters of the law. His use of the word 'spiritual' is used to make the readers aware that God's commandments that were prescribed only to the Jewish nation of Israel (not to the gentiles), are of a spiritual nature (which only Jesus was able to fully and completely fulfill) and are perfect, *"The law of the Lord is perfect, converting the soul, Psalm19:7.* The law may be able to convert the soul, but it can never bring life, *"Is the law then against the promises of God? Certainly not! For if there had been a law given which could have **given life**, truly righteousness would have been by the law. But the scripture has **confined all under sin,** that the promise by faith in Jesus Christ might be given to those who **believe," Galatians 3:21,22.*

The 'promise' stated in the above scripture is the promise Jesus stated over and over; eternal life in heaven to whoever believes in Him. We know that the law is spiritual because the law can only be fulfilled within the spiritual realm, or in other words by Jesus Himself. How could a person who is not born-again in his spirit completely and perfectly fulfill the law?

To grasp the fully completed work of Christ, it is important to know how his death on the cross completely satisfied the requirements of the law. We must also understand that these passages of scripture were written after the Apostle Paul was born-again, filled with the God's Holy Spirit and infused with the knowledge of God by Jesus Himself, *"For I would have you know brethren, that the gospel which was preached by me is not according to man. For I neither received it from man, nor was I taught it, but **I received it through a revelation of Jesus Christ**,"* Galatians 1:11,12 (NAS).

This means that the Apostle Paul wrote these passages from the vantage point of already knowing and understanding the reality of what he was going through and what other born-again believers would go through concerning the spiritual conflict that he himself was experiencing. As the Apostle Paul continues his writing, he does so with total absolute clarity of his condition prior to being born-again and his condition after being born-again.

"but I am of the flesh, sold under sin." Here the Apostle Paul is using the word 'flesh' in the context of his flesh being the totality of who and what he is; body, soul and spirit prior to being born-again. He is declaring that he understands the totality of his sinfulness and of him being a slave to it. Paul is also stating a covenant fact. He, along with all humanity, were given over to Satan at the Garden of Eden through Adam and Eve's sinful act of disobedience to God.

For I do not understand my own actions. The apostle Paul is expressing to us what is taking place between his physical actions and the reasoning processes of his immaterial mind. Again, we see the triune nature of humanity; 'I' is his 'spirit' (being alive), understanding is taking place in his soul-consciousness-mind and his actions are done by his body. He is engaged in using his mental reasoning powers, in his soul/mind to try to comprehend his fleshly behaviors, that were not only contrary to his desires, but also to God's will.

Before his born-again conversion, there was no need for the Apostle Paul to try to understand his behaviors, he believed that what he was thinking, saying and doing was not sinful and was what God wanted Him to do. After his conversion and revelation from Jesus Christ, the Apostle Paul understood the reality of his sinfulness and his total inability to make himself the 'new creation' that he had been changed into by the sacrifice of Jesus and the infilling of the Holy Spirit.

For I do not do what I want, but I do the very thing I hate. The Apostle Paul at this point almost sounds schizophrenic, almost as if someone or something is forcing him to do the things he has no desire to do. He is stating that he is fully cognizant that what he (in his spirit) wants to do, what his mind (soul) tells him he should do and what he desires to do, he does *not do*, but rather the opposite he does, how miserable this must be for the great Apostle Paul. The very thing he hates (sin), he does. He is fully aware of how his soul and flesh are not only in disagreement with what he ('I-spirit') desires (soul), but that his soul and flesh (body) also have the ability to overtake the desires of his spirit.

Now if I do what I do not want, I agree with the law, that it is good. Who knows more about the law than the Apostle Paul. He made it a point to the Jews that he was extremely knowledgeable about the Law, *"If anyone else has a mind to put confidence in the flesh, I far more: circumcised on the eighth day, of the nation of Israel, of the tribe of Benjamin, a Hebrew of Hebrews; as to the Law, a Pharisee; as to zeal, a persecutor of the church; as to the righteousness which is in the Law, found blameless. But whatever things were gain to me, those things I have counted as loss for the sake of Christ," Philippians 3:4-7 (NAS).* Here he is stating that he, the great Apostle Paul, is engaging in behaviors that are sinful and unlawful and that although he is doing them, he himself does not want to do them.

The law he is writing about is the holy law of God, the commandments of God and not the law of sin and death. The law of sin and death is, internal and within the human body, *soul and spirit* of every non-born-again person. It is inescapable to them who are without the saving grace of Jesus.

For every born-again believer, however, the law of sin and death is still incurable to the flesh, and irrelevant or of no consequence to the spirit and soul. In this passage, the Apostle Paul begins to tell us that he agrees that the law of God is good, even though he is fully aware that he himself breaks the law and cannot keep the entirety of the law, but instead does what it is the law tells him not to do.

So now it is no longer I who do it, but sin that dwells within me. It almost sounds as if the great Apostle Paul was suffering from a mental disorder when he wrote this passage and, as you will see, some of the passages to follow, instead the opposite is true. He has been given knowledge about the realities of the visible and invisible worlds that simultaneously exist, and the reality of what we, as humans, are composed of, to pass on that knowledge for our benefit.

It is at this juncture that the apostle Paul begins to put into effect Hebrews 4:12, *"The word of God is active and sharper than any two-edged sword, and piercing as far as the division of <u>soul</u> and <u>spirit</u>, of both <u>joints and marrow</u>," (NAS),* which is a picture of the triune composition of humanity; body, soul and spirit. The apostle Paul is fully aware of the nature of humanity and the power and dwelling place of sin; the flesh and the soul. He makes the distinction between 'I' and the 'sin' that dwells within him, that is within his flesh but also in his mind for his, as well as our minds, need to be renewed, *"…in reference to your former manner of life, you lay aside the old self, which is being corrupted in accordance with the lusts of deceit, and that you be renewed in the spirit of your mind, and put on the new self, which in the likeness of God has been created in righteousness and holiness of the truth," Ephesians 4:22-24.*

For I know that nothing good dwells within me, that is in my flesh.
Paul is now clarifying the previous statement that the 'nothing good' that
dwells within him, dwells in his flesh (joints and marrow), not in who and
what he really is-spirit! It is clear to the apostle Paul that his sinful acts are
acts done by him, however, not only through the power of his flesh but also
through that part of his mind which has not been completely renewed, for
the renewal of the mind is a life-long process that never reaches full
completion until we stand face to face with Christ.

He now starts to make his argument that although he is the one doing
the sinning, the 'nothing good' that is in him is not who he really is. The
'nothing good,' that dwells within him is who he *was*! He is aware of the
dichotomy of his personhood. "It is no longer 'my spirit' who does it, but sin
that dwells within my flesh' is another way to state the above scripture.

For I have the desire to do what is right, but not the ability to carry it
out. Once again; 'I'-spirit, 'desire'-soul, and 'ability'-body. What true born-
again believer does not have the desire to do what is right in God's sight?
At this point the inner-man, or the 'I,' (Paul's spirit) as Paul rightly refers
himself to, does not have the ability to do what he knows is right. The
Apostle Paul is no longer talking about the subject of the reality of his sinful
flesh. He has now focused on the inner man-his spirit, the real him, the
one who wants to do right, but is totally incapable of doing what he knows
to be the right thing to do. What the Apostle Paul begins to build here is
the fact that he, himself, by himself, has absolutely no ability to do Godly

righteous acts. He begins, at this point, removing all possible credit for any righteous act he may perform.

For I do not do the good I want, but the evil I do not want is what I keep on doing. There are three distinct issues here; the first is the fact that the Apostle Paul knows that he does not do the 'good' that he wants to do. The second is the antithesis of the good he wants to do, which is the evil that he continues to do and third is the fact that he continues doing the very thing he does not want to do!

Now if I do what I do not want, it is no longer I who do it, but sin that dwells within me. At first glance, it appears that the Apostle Paul is trying to thwart off the blame for his sinful actions rather than taking responsibility for his own actions. In this passage, the great Apostle Paul begins to explain this dilemma that he finds himself entangled in. He begins by declaring that he is aware of behaving in a manner that is totally contrary to his desire.

'I' expressed three times in this passage refers to the Apostle Paul's spirit, the real him, that is doing what he, the great Apostle Paul, does not want to do, which, his body and soul, however, continually do by moving towards getting what they want, crave for and demand even when the Apostle Paul knows that he does not want to do it. Here we have a great distinction between the 'spirit' of who and what a born-again believer truly is and the sin nature that was once who and what he was before his conversion.

In spite of being co-joined with his sinful body and sinful soul the born-again believer's spirit, that has been spiritually separate from his sinful material body and the sinful immaterial soul, can now begin to grow in the grace and mercy of God knowing that his sins committed while working towards doing God's will, will never be held against him, *"Blessed are those whose **lawless deeds** are **forgiven**, And whose **sins** are **covered**; Blessed is the man to whom the Lord shall **not impute sin**,"* Romans 4:7,8. The analogy would be like an American citizen who becomes an Ambassador and is living in another country that he has been appointed to by the U.S. Government. The United States Ambassador has the legal weight of the United States of America behind him and although he is living in another country he is not part of that country nor is he bound by their laws and has immunity from the consequences of breaking any of their laws. So, it is, with the spirit of a born-again believer.

A born-again believer's spirit is separated spiritually from their sinful nature (soul and body) at the time of their rebirth or their born-again conversion, *"In Him you were also circumcised with the circumcision made without hands, by putting off **the body** of the sins of the flesh, by the circumcision of Christ,"* Colossians 2:11. *"For the word of God is living and powerful, and sharper than any two-edged sword piercing even to the **division of soul and spirit**, and of **joints and marrow**,"* Hebrews 4:12.

This separation is not only essential but also sufficient to the purpose of fulfilling the mystery of God, that is Christ, the one and only true living God, creator of the heavenly realms and our physical universe living in the believer's spirit, *"the mystery which has been hidden from ages and from* *generations, but now has been revealed to His saints. To them God willed to make known what are the riches of the glory of this **mystery** among the Gentiles: which is **Christ in you,** the hope of glory," Colossians 1:26, 27.*

It is of utmost importance to understand that upon a believer's conversion their sinful (soul/consciousness/mind) nature remains intact within their physical material body, but not within their immaterial spirit or in other words the body and soul continue to be what they were prior to the spirit being born-again. God will not reside with sin, for He is a Holy God and for this reason he separates our spirit from our soul and body in order for Him to live in our spirit, as we live in Him for the purpose of becoming one with Him, while we are still living in this world, *"I do not pray for these alone, but also for those who will believe in Me through their word; that they all may be one, as You Father, are **in Me,** and **I in You;** that **they** also may be **one in Us,** John 17:20,21.*

If we do not take into account the sinfulness of our soul and all that it is made of there can be much confusion concerning things of the soul; desires, freewill, reasoning, intelligence, emotions, etc.... Our soul lies in-between our spirit and our body and is the entity that we use to decide what it is we are going to do at any given time. When we make up our minds to do something, it is the 'I' (spirit) part of us that makes up our mind (soul) to do (body) the very thing we have decided to do.

So I find it to be a law that when I want to do right, evil lies close at hand. This law that Paul finds is not within the natural physical realm, but instead this law of sin and death lies within the immaterial world of consciousness and expressed within the flesh and material world. In the same manner that the law of gravity exerts its power, 'Want' is the power that pulls us towards acquiring the object of what it is we want when we want it, whether good or bad, right or wrong, moral or immoral. This law is simply the way our immaterial soul/consciousness works in this created physical universe.

The Apostle Paul is informing us of the reality of the evil that lives next to every one of us. He can only know this truth if he is born of God. Anyone who is not born of God, cannot discern good from evil, but here the Apostle Paul who is obviously born-again begins to inform us of the reality of the law of sin. He is fully aware of the fact that he himself has been separated from his own immaterial evil nature that lies within his own fleshly body and immaterial soul.

The reason that he can write that "evil lies close," is that evil continues to live in that part of what and who he *was*, physically (body) and consciously (soul) prior to his born-again conversion, however, he is now an Ambassador to his own body and soul but is no longer part of that country nor is he bound by their laws. He is now a new creation of God! His spirit is born-again, his soul is in the process of sanctification and his body is dead-period!

His evil nature (not demons, Satan or the world), nevertheless is permanently there, within his flesh and mind to pull him back to do what he has no desire to do. In the same way that when we throw an object up in the air, gravity is there to pull it back from where it rested, so it is when we desire to do God's will, evil is there to pull us back towards our old evil self from which we were spiritually delivered from at the time of our conversion, *"For He **delivered us from the domain of darkness**, and transferred us to the kingdom of His Beloved Son, in whom we have redemption, the forgiveness of sins, Colossians 1:13 (NAS).*

We must remember that even though born-again believers have been delivered from the kingdom of darkness, their old self <u>continues</u> to become corrupted, *"lay aside the old self, which is **being corrupted** in accordance with the lusts of deceit," Ephesians 4:22.* Notice that the scripture states that the old self is '*being corrupted*,' not *was* corrupted or has ceased from corruption. This is because our old self will always be in direct opposition to our new self. While the new self, with the presence and power of the Holy Spirit within our born-again spirit, influences our soul; personality, desires, reasoning, mind, etc....towards sanctification. The old self fights hard, not only to stop our spiritual growth, but to get us to renounce our faith and our walk with the Lord.

For I delight in the <u>law of God,</u> in my inner being; Notice here how the Apostle Paul makes it a point to emphasize that it is his 'inner being,' or to put it another way, his born-again spirit, that delights in the law of God. His body and his 'old self, way of thinking have not been regenerated or born-again.

...but I see in my members <u>another law </u>waging war against the law of my mind... It is important to understand the function and position of the soul/mind, so we may get a good understanding of this passage of scripture.   Here we have the trinity of man; the born-again spirit that delights in God's law, the members or the physical parts of the body and the mind that is implanted not in the body or spirit, but in the soul.

Remember that the mind is always in a state of growth towards either the things of God or the things of the world. The mind enables us to say 'yes' to God or 'yes' to the things of the world. The born-again believer can be transformed through the renewing of their mind, *"Be transformed by the renewing of your mind," Romans 12:2.* Thus, the mind is what will be pulled by the lustful desires of the body as well as the influence of Satan and the way of the world, to get what it WANTS! Paul is clear in depicting the conflict he is experiencing; the law of God, in which his inner man delights, versus the law of his members (his flesh/body), fighting for the functioning and dominion of his mind or the "law" of his "mind."

It is in the mind that we decide to follow the leading of the Holy Spirit or give in to the lusts of the flesh or of the world. So, we have here the law of God, which is that law that is within his born-again spirit and the law waging war against his mind that is within his flesh, but also within part of his consciousness (soul/mind) or in his old way of thinking. The Apostle Paul's soul, along with his flesh prior to his conversion, was completely and totally evil and without any inclination to do God's will. He only believed he was doing God's will, even while sending born-again believers to their death. He knew nothing of God or His will, he only had a humanistic point of view of God's law, to which he counted as rubbish, in comparison to knowing Christ after his conversion.

and making me captive to <u>the law of sin</u> that dwells in my members. The law of sin is imbedded within the flesh, the consciousness and the spirit of humanity, it wants what it wants when it wants it!! The Apostle Paul is fully aware of his predicament and his imprisonment to his own body, that not only knows and only wants to sin, but is also completely and totally contrary to God's will. The Apostle Paul, however, is baiting us in, for the purpose of coming to a most excellent conclusion; He (we) is wretched and he knows it! His next statement is really a rhetorical declaration for he is completely aware of the solution to his problem.

Wretched man that I am! Who will deliver me from this body of death?" Romans 7:14-24 (ESV). Here, the Apostle Paul first cries out a declaration of truth; he is absolutely and totally a wretched man! He is fully aware of what and who he truly is, no question about it! He also represents the whole of humanity, for we are all wretched. The second part of this verse is a rhetorical question. He already knows the answer because it was revealed to him by Jesus Himself (Galatians 1:12).

The above scriptures lead up to this final declaration about the absolute truth concerning humanities condition and poses the question; "who will deliver me (us) from this body of death?"

"I thank God-through Jesus Christ our Lord!" Romans 7:25.

"There is none righteous, not even one; There is none who understands, there is none who seeks after God; All have turned aside, together they

have become useless; There is none who does good, no, there is not even one," Romans 3:10-12. "Moreover, the law entered that the offense might abound. But **where sin abounded, grace abounded much more**, so that as sin reigned in death, even so **grace might reign through righteousness to eternal life through <u>Jesus Christ our Lord</u>**," Romans 5:20,21.

CHAPTER 8
THE SEPARATION OF SOUL AND SPIRIT

"For the word of God is living and powerful, and sharper than any two-edged sword, piercing even to the division of soul and spirit," Hebrews 4:12.

The soul, as we have learned, is immaterial and influenced by both earthly and heavenly things and events. It must be renewed through the word of God, and the working of the Holy Spirit, daily. The soul encompasses a person's; freewill, consciousness, mind, emotions, desires, thoughts, beliefs, feelings of love, hate, joy, depression, etc. The soul of a true born-again believer is always in the process of being transformed, being sanctified, being perfected and being made holy through the use of our freewill and desire (soul) to be more Christ like.

It is because of the soul's imperfect state and its intertwined relationship with the world, worldly friends, Satan's power and his/her own personal sinful unregenerate body that it needs to be separated from our spirit, *"For the word of God is living and powerful, and sharper than any*

two- edged sword, piercing even to the **division of soul and spirit**,"
Hebrews 4:12.

The physical body is separated from the immaterial soul and spirit at death, however the soul and spirit, which are immaterial and eternal in both the unsaved and saved person are co-existent and eternal. Once the spirit has been regenerated through the born-again experience, it is perfect, sanctified and made holy by the infilling of the Holy Spirit.

The spirit that is born-again unto eternal salvation will never be 'unborn' to be born-again over and over every time sin is committed. Why? Because the infilling of the Holy Spirit is an *eternal gift* and a *guarantee* of our eternal salvation, which can never be taken away from you, "*In Him you also trusted, after you heard the word of truth, the gospel of your salvation; in who also having believed, you were **sealed with the Holy Spirit** of promise, who is the **guarantee** of our inheritance until the redemption of the purchased possession, to the praise of His glory,*" Ephesians 1:13-14.

Upon regeneration, the spirit and the soul are separated, obviously not in a physical sense, but through a spiritual act of God. The regenerated perfect and sanctified spirit is now one with the Father, Son and Holy Spirit. The soul, however, is and always will be, in need of, and in the process of being sanctified. This is clearly seen by the sinful thoughts and acts we continue to do, but now hate to do, rather than love to do; "*For what I am doing I do not understand. For what I will to do, that I do not practice but **what I hate, that I do**...Now if I do what I will not to do, it is no longer I who do it, but sin that dwells in me,*" Romans 7:15-17.

This may be hard to understand, but your spirit can no longer sin because it has been born-again; *"**Whoever** has been **born of God does not sin,** for His seed remains in him and **he cannot sin, because he has been born of God,**"* 1John 3:9, *"**having been born-again** not of corruptible seed but incorruptible, through the word of God which lives and abides forever…,"* 1 Peter 1:23. It is through our soul that the seed of sin begins to grow, depending on the thought patterns of that person, believer or non-believer. This is where most Christians fail in their understanding of their true born-again condition. Every born-again believer needs to understand that they are perfect in God's sight *in their spirit-period!* And although we are not perfect in our soul, we, nevertheless, are accepted and loved by God because as "far as east is from west," our sins been removed from us.

It is like our sinful soul is on a different dimensional plane than the dimensional plane from where our perfect spirit resides. No one needs to tell us that we sin in our soul/mind. If we are truly 'born-again' Christians, then we are fully aware of how sinful our own thoughts can be. That is why it is our soul/mind that will undergo the continual process of sanctification, but not the spirit. Case in point; *"It is actually reported that there is sexual immorality among you, and such sexual immorality as is not even named among the Gentiles – that a **man has his father's wife**! And you are puffed up, and have not rather mourned, that he who has done this deed might be taken away from among you. "For I indeed, as absent in body but present in spirit, have already judged (as though I were present) him who has so done this deed. In the name of our Lord Jesus Christ, when you are* *gathered together, along with my spirit, with the power of our Lord Jesus Christ, deliver such a one to Satan for the **destruction of the flesh**, that his **spirit may be saved** in the day of the Lord Jesus,"* 1 Corinthians 5:1-5.

Now this indeed is a very strange incident that needs close attention. By now we should understand that we are a triune being; body, soul and spirit. Here in this passage mentioned above we can clearly see what is happening in the body, soul and spirit of the man involved in this sexually immoral relationship. Physically, the man is involved in a sin of a sexual nature with a person, that even by today's standards would be utterly despicable. That is what this man, using his freewill, (soul-mind) desired to do.

The apostle Paul's reaction to this scenario that is happening in the "church of God," as strange as it may sound, falls in line with the gospel message of Christ that he has been, for many years, preaching and is found throughout the New Testament. But before we assess his reaction, let's recap some of the things we've learned concerning the triune nature of man.

First, let us consider the body; *"it is the spirit that gives life, the **flesh counts for nothing**."* Second, the soul; *"For the word of God is living and powerful, and sharper than any two-edged sword, piercing even to the **division of soul** and spirit, and of joints and marrow, and is a discerner of the **thoughts and intents of the heart**,* Hebrews 4:12. *"Beloved, I pray that you may prosper in all things and be in health, just as your **soul prospers**,"* 3 John 1:2 Thirdly, the spirit; *"That which is born of the flesh is flesh and that which is **born of the Spirit is spirit**,"* *"Unless one is born* *again, he cannot see the kingdom of God," "Most assuredly, I say to you, unless on is born of water and* **the Spirit***, he cannot enter the kingdom of God John 3:3,5.*

God's will for the whole person; body-soul-spirit, is to be found blameless. *"Now may the God of peace Himself sanctify you completely; and may your whole* **spirit, soul, and body** *be preserved blameless at the coming of our Lord Jesus Christ," 2 Thessalonians 5:23.* Remember in Chapter 2 the Thief who made it into paradise with Jesus. Well, we have a similar case here. This man is just as despicable as the thief, however, this man, who has his father's wife, is not tied to a cross and at death's doorstep. This scenario, like that of the 'Thief,' also carries with it theological implications.

One of the most obvious is the fact that the apostle Paul did not inform the church members, to whom he was addressing, to tell this man to confess his sin! 'Get this man to confess his sin so he can get right with God!' How many of us have heard this line in church!? Where in the New Testament will you find scripture telling born-again believers to '*continually' confess* their sins so they can get right and stay right with God? "Nowhere!!" CONFESS JESUS is what you will find, NOT confessing SINS!! We are called to CONFESS JESUS, not sins!

Why do we need to confess our sins to Him who knows every little thing we do, on a minute by minute basis? *"Also, I say to you, whoever* **confesses Me** *before men, Him the Son of Man also will confess before the angels of God," Luke 12:8.* Rather than confessing that you stole, steal no more! If you committed adultery-commit adultery no more, if you lied-lie no more! That is why the Bible tells us to stop sinning if we are sinning, rather than confessing our sin of stealing, *"Let him who stole **steal no longer**, but rather let him labor, working with his hands what is good, that he may have something to give who has need, Ephesians 4:28.* This would be a good place to interject the 'confessing of sins,' however, there is no mention of confessing the sin of stealing.

Jesus never mentioned or commanded anyone to confess their sins. In fact, He gave rather a stark alternative to confessing our sins, *"If your right eye causes you to sin, **pluck it out** and cast it from you,"* Matthew 5:30. Wouldn't you agree that this would be a good place to hear; *"confess your sin"* rather than plucking out an eye? Why didn't Jesus just command us to confess our sin rather than to pluck out our eye if it causes us to sin? Why didn't the apostle Paul tell the apostle Peter to confess his sin of leading other church members astray with his hypocritical behavior (see Galatians chapter 2). Also, why didn't the apostle Paul tell the church members in the church at Corinth to tell the person who had his father's wife to confess his sin?

There are Literally dozens and dozens of verses throughout the New Testament where telling someone to confess their sin would seem to be the most appropriate and expedient thing for the person sinning to do, however, the opposite is what you will find. Why is this so? That is because it is the unregenerate body and the *'in the process of sanctification soul,'* of the *believer* that is doing the sinning. The Bible is clear about the nature of man-we sin! The great men of God sinned before, during and after the ministry of Christ Jesus. However, it is for this purpose that the Son of Man was manifested; to take away the sin of the world! *"And you know that He was manifested to* **take away our sins** *and in Him there is no sin, 1 John 3:5.*

Jesus took care of the sin issue. What takes place in the soul/mind is the process of sanctification. For the believer, the body is dead, but the spirit is perfect and filled with the God's Holy Spirit, while the, 'in the process of being sanctified soul/mind,' decides which to follow, the desires of the flesh or the leading of the Holy Spirit living in their spirit. The believer's body cannot be anymore dead than it already is because its destination is absolute and final – the grave! The body is always in the process of dying, aging, decaying until death arrives. The destination of the believer's spirit is also absolute and final-heaven! There is no need to sanctify the spirit for God's presence sanctifies and makes holy and perfect a person's spirit the moment they become 'born-again'! *"for by one offering, He has perfected, forever, those who are being sanctified,"* Hebrews 10:14

The ability to see the kingdom of God does not start in heaven, it starts here on earth because the kingdom of God is within every born-again believer's spirit; *"Now when He was asked by the Pharisees when the kingdom of God would come, He answered them and said, "The kingdom of God does not come with observation; "nor will they say, 'See here!' or 'See there!' For indeed, the* ***kingdom of God is within you****,"* Luke 17:20.

It is obvious that the kingdom of God is not within our soul, Romans chapter 7 clearly depicts the nature of the born-again believer's soul, and the great apostle Paul was a born-again believer. True born-again believers know they sin. The purpose for the division of the soul from spirit is for the process of sanctification of the soul, not of the spirit, for the spirit of every born-again believer was sanctified and perfected at the point of conversion.

It is the soul that mediates between what the physical body will do in this physical world when prompted by the leading of the Holy Spirit in the spiritual realm. This process cannot even start to take place until there is a division between our soul and our spirit, or in other words, until one is 'born-again.' In the book of Luke, Jesus told a parable of two men, one a Pharisee and one a Tax Collector, who went to the temple to pray.

In the following parable Jesus tells us that a Pharisee believed, he himself, was righteous because of his good works/behaviors; *"God, I thank You that I am not like other men - extortioners, unjust, adulterers, or even as this tax collector. I fast twice a week; I give tithes of all that I possess.' And the tax collector, standing off, would not so much as raise his eyes to heaven, but beat his breast, saying, "God be merciful to me a sinner!' Luke 18:11-13.* Jesus stated that the Tax Collector was justified before God rather than the Pharisee. Jesus at the end of the Parable then adds; *"for everyone who exalts himself will be humbled, and he who humbles himself will be exalted," Luke 18: 10-14.*

Imagine that!? A 'man of the cloth (a Pharisee),' not only praying to God (how righteous that must look to those standing around), but rather confessing, not his sins, but instead his good righteous godly works as well as declaring to God that he was not like the sinful tax collector. The tax collector also did NOT confess his sins, but rather confessed that he was a sinner, for he knew he was not even worthy to look up towards heaven.

Instead he beat his breast, saying, 'God be merciful to me a sinner!' How interesting that even though both men did not confess their sins, one of them walked away *justified before God*; the 'tax collector,' who knew he was a sinner and not even worthy of looking up to the heavens.

In the days of the New Testament, tax collectors were considered by the people, to be 'thieves' sanctioned by the ruling authorities. How about that, another thief! Both thieves depicted in the Bible did not confess their sins (if you remember, not seven the thief on the cross confessed his sins before making it in into paradise with Jesus). Why are these people in the New Testament getting away with their sins? The answer is that they are not. No one gets away with sinning. Sinning begins in the mind, can stay in the mind (feasting on an ungodly thought), or be manifested through the body by the acting out of sinful thoughts. But remember, 'the wages of sin, is death,' however, Jesus paid the price for the sins of the world!

We know, most of the time, when we are sinning, God knows when we are sinning *all the time*, but we don't know when we are sinning in ignorance. The knowing or not knowing when we sin takes place within the confines of the mind/soul. What does a person do with the sins they commit in ignorance? If you believe that you need to confess every sin you commit, then what do you do with the sins you commit in ignorance?

In the Old Testament, God addressed sins committed in ignorance; *"And if anyone of the common people sin through ignorance, while he doeth somewhat against any of the commandments of the Lord concerning things which ought not to be done, and be guilty; or if his sin, which he hath sinned, come to his knowledge: then he shall bring his offering, a kid of the goats, a female without blemish, for his sin which he hath sinned, Leviticus 4:27 (KJV).* So, obliviously there are sins we commit that we are not even aware of. How do we confess what we know not?

There is no hope for humanity if we are left to ourselves to get right with God by confessing our sins to Him. However, once we grasp the reality that Jesus died for *all our sins*, past-present-future, those committed purposefully and those committed in ignorance, then we can start to understand the purpose of our soul needing to be separated from our spirit.

It is imperative for believers to understand and appreciate God's holy word that declares they are perfect and sanctified even though they know they still sin. Let's take a closer look at scripture to get a better understanding of sin, the nature of humanity and the reason God's word tells us that the soul and spirit are divided; *"This is the message which we have heard from Him and declare to you, that God is light and in Him is no darkness at all. "If we say that we have fellowship with Him, and walk in the darkness, we lie and do not practice the truth. But if we walk in the light as He is in the light, we have fellowship with the one another, and the blood of Jesus Christ His Son cleanses us from* **all** *sin. If we say that we have no sin, we deceive ourselves, and the truth is not in us. If we* **confess ours sins**, *He is faithful and just to forgive us our sins, and to* **cleans us from all** *unrighteousness. If we say the we have not sinned, we make him a liar, and His word is not in us," "My little children, these things I write to you,* **so that you may not sin**. *And* **if anyone sins, we have an Advocate** *with the Father, Jesus Christ the righteous," 1 John 1:5-10.*

First, it is Jesus, who John has heard this message from. What is the message? 'That God is light and in Him there is no darkness.' What darkness is he talking about? The darkness of sin (not having the light of God in their spirit-being born-again) because God is sinless. When God's Holy Spirit (God's light) comes to live inside the (dark-unilluminated) *spirit* of the believer, all darkness (sin) is eradicated and the spirit is completely and totally sin free (illuminated-fill with His light-His presence) and cannot sin because God's presence does not allow sin to come in. This is the first step of what Jesus' sacrifice on the cross, for the sins of the world, has accomplish for God the Father to do, *"God was in Christ **reconciling** the world to Himself, **not imputing their trespasses to them**,"* 2 Corinthians *5:19.*

There are many people who profess to be Christians, but if they are not born-again or '*walking in the light*,' they lie. A person can only '*walk in the light*,' with God, if they are born-again. Only born-again believers walk in the light and have no darkness in their *spirit*. Every born-again believer also knows that there is sin (darkness) in their body and in their soul. That is what Romans chapter 7 clearly states; *"For what I am doing, I do not understand. For what **I will** to do, that I do not practice; but what I hate that I do. If, then, I do what **I will** not to do, I agree with the law that it is good. But now, it is no longer I who do it, but sin that dwells in me. For I know that in me (that is in **my flesh**) nothing good dwells; for **to will** is present with me, but how to perform what is good I do not find…Romans 7:15-18.*

In this chapter, the apostle Paul is clearly stating that he knows the depravity of his body and his soul (freewill). He gives us the remedy for our sinful situation at the end of chapter 7; *"O wretched man that I am! Who will deliver me from this body of death? "I thank God – through Jesus Christ our Lord! So then, with the mind (soul) I (spirt) myself serve the law of God, but with the flesh (body), the law of sin,"* Romans 7:24,25.

He then begins to clarify in chapter 8, the reality of those who are in Christ Jesus; *"So, then, those who are in the flesh **(not saved or not born-again)** cannot please God. **But you are not in the flesh but in the Spirit**, if indeed the Spirit of God dwells in you. Now if anyone does not have the Spirit of Christ, he is not His. And if Christ is in you, the **body is dead because of sin**, but the **Spirit is life** because of righteousness,"* Romans 8:8-10. *"But **you** are **not in the flesh** but **in the Spirit**,"* clearly elucidates the reality of where the born-again believer resides; not in his body (flesh), but rather in his spirit, where God resides, as stated' *"**if** indeed the Spirit of God dwells in you."*

This is the invisible, immaterial, spiritual aspect of the believer's life; *"The wind blows where it wishes, and you hear the sound of it, but **cannot tell where it comes from and where it goes**. So is **everyone who is born of the Spirit**,"* John3:8. When a nonbeliever sees the physical body of a believer, the nonbeliever cannot discern anything spiritual about the believer.

Over and over throughout the New Testament the flesh and the spirit are always in contrast to one another in the life of the believer. There is nothing that they have in common – absolutely nothing! The soul however, is usually implied throughout scripture because it is the 'mind' of those in the New Testament as well as those to whom scripture is addressing - the reader of scripture, when discussing the flesh and the spirit. This is important to understand, if we are to grasp what 'confessing' our sins, means in 1 John 1:9.

The first order of business is to look at ALL of verse 9, not just the 'confess our sins' part, and we must do this with the understanding of the entire message of the gospel of Jesus Christ in the New Testament. Let's look at *"He is faithful and just to forgive us our sins and to cleanse us from* **all** *unrighteousness,"* which is stated immediately after "confess our sins."

What is Jesus faithful to? He is faithful to His new covenant that was appropriated by his shed blood and death for the *sins of the world*. He is now eternally faithful and *'just to forgive us of our sins AND to cleanse us from ALL unrighteousness.'* He is faithful to always forgive and cleanse us from all sin (willful sins and *sins done in ignorance*), always and forever.

We can take this information two ways; First, the sacrifice of Christ on the cross forgave and cleansed us from ALL sin 'once and for all,' or second, the sacrifice of Christ is *continually* forgiving us and cleansing the believer from ALL sin. Jesus is the one who does the forgiving and the cleansing of ALL past-present-future sins. That is why the apostle Paul did not tell the man who had his father's wife to confess his sin to be forgiven and cleansed from his sin. That man's body was as dead as the next person, however, his 'spirit' was saved and utterly and completely free from sin. It was his soul, his conscious mind, his freewill and desires that needed to be sanctified or renewed. That is why the apostle Paul did not ask the church to tell that man to confess his sins, the believer's sins are ALWAYS forgiven and ALWAYS cleansed; *"If I do not **wash you**, you have*

no part with Me," John 13:8. "Behold, I have come to do Your will, O God."
He takes away the first that He may establish the second. By that will we
have been sanctified *through the offering of the body of Jesus Christ*
once for all," *Hebrews 10:10. "But this Man, after He had offered one*
sacrifice for sins forever, sat down at the right hand of God, from that time
waiting till His enemies are made His footstool. For by one offering He has
perfected forever *those who are* **being sanctified***." Hebrews 10:14.*

There is no contradiction in the above scriptures, the *'perfected*
forever' spirit *has been* sanctified, the soul *is being* sanctified.' It is the duty
of every born-again believer to sanctify or set apart their soul/mind to the
will of God, while they are alive here on earth with the knowledge God's
Holy Spirit, resides within their spirit. So how does 'confessing' your sins
make you more perfect than you already are in God's eyes or more
forgiven than you already are? Why is 'confessing' your sin needed when
Jesus has 'once and for all' offered Himself as a sacrifice for sins 'forever?'
"Confessing your sins, referred to in 1 John 1:9, is really the confession
unto salvation or in other words what a sinner does when he confesses that
he is a sinner and in need of Jesus. Like the sinner who could not even
look up to heaven and just beat his breast and said, "God be merciful to
me, a sinner," Luke 18:13.

When a person acknowledges that he is a sinner and accepts Jesus
as Lord and Savior, he is completely cleansed and forgiven of ALL past-
present-future sins. If we must confess our sins to get right with God, we
will never get right with God, due to the fact that we also sin in ignorance-
we cannot get away from this fact. Thank God, He has taken care of every

sin we have done, are doing and will do in the future, the sins we know we have done, the sins we have forgotten that we have done and the sins we don't even know are sins, otherwise, there would be absolutely no hope for mankind.

There is also another reason why we do not need to confess our sins daily, as some believe. God does not want to know or remember our sins; *"For this is the **new covenant** that I will make with the house of Israel after those days, say the Lord: I will put My laws in their mind and write them on their hearts; and I will be their God, and they shall be my peoples. None of them shall teach his neighbor, and none his brother, saying know the Lord, for all shall know Me, from the least of them to the greatest of them. For I will be merciful to their unrighteousness, and their **sins and lawless deeds I will remember no more,***" Hebrews 8:10-12.

What we have here is God telling us that He will no longer remember our sins because of His mercy towards us. He demonstrated that mercy by the giving of His only begotten Son, Jesus. *"For as high as the heavens are above the earth, so great is his love for those who fear Him; **as far as east is from the west, so far has he removed our transgressions from us**. As a father has compassion on his children, so the Lord has compassion on those who fear him; for he knows how we are formed, he remembers that we are dust, Psalm 103:11-14.* In this scripture, God is telling us that He 'knows' how we are formed and 'remembers' that we are but dust, but also declares that our sins have been removed from us and so removed are they from us that the statement; 'as far as east is from west' is used to convey that fact.

We know that because of God's holiness and righteousness He will not reside with sin. However, because of Christ's perfect sacrifice for the removal of our sins we can live our lives knowing that our *spirit*, that has been divided and separated from our soul, is perfect and holy in His eyes.

The moment a person becomes 'born-again,' his/her spirit is made alive and perfect in every way. That is the condition that a person's spirit must be in, for God's Holy Spirit to come and reside within that person's spirit. Without this understanding, it will be easy to call yourself a failure, live in penance (always paying for your own sins by engaging in 'works' or sufferings) and/or live in a miserable state of self-deprecation.

God has chosen to deem you ('I'-spirit) perfect, sanctified and holy not because of any thing you've done or could do, but rather because you have "believed," in Him, whom He has sent-Jesus! For it is by 'believing' that one is credited with righteousness, *"Abraham **believed God**, and it was counted to him as righteousness. Now to the one who works, his wages are not counted as a gift but as his due. And to the one who does not work but **believes** in Him who justifies, his faith is counted as righteousness, Romans 4:3-5 (ESV).* It is a spiritual necessity that our spirit and soul be separated.

Once again, what has been perfected forever? our spirit! What is *being* sanctified as you read this? your soul! What is unredeemable at all times? your body. And that is why; *"There is therefore, **no more condemnation** for **those who are in Christ Jesus**,"* Romans 8:1.

CHAPTER 9

THE PERFECT- IMPERFECT MAN

"For by one offering He has perfected forever those who are being sanctified," Hebrews 10:14.

How can a person be perfect and sanctified and be in the process of 'being perfected and sanctified,' at the same time? It sounds illogical because nothing in this physical realm can 'be perfect' and *not* 'be perfect' at the same time and in the same sense. However, from a theistic worldview; *"with God, all things are possible," Matthew 19:26.*

At this point in the book we should already have a pretty good idea of our triune nature; body, soul and spirit. Once we understand that we are a triune being, consisting of three distinct different entities, it should be easy to grasp the idea that these three distinct entities; body, soul and spirit are not the same thing. If they were, then they would be one and the same and we would either be all matter with no immaterial aspect to who we are, or in other words we would be mindless, random moving, conglomerates of atoms and molecules, no different than a rock or a mud puddle, or we would be only nonphysical, formless consciousness.

We, however, know (*coming to know something* is an immaterial conscious act) that we have an immaterial soul/spirit along with our material body and that our mind responds in ways that are not identical to our physical body. When a person has a stroke, for instance, their stroke may have incapacitated a certain area of their body. The person who had the stroke knows he cannot move that part of his body, but wants and tries desperately to move it, but cannot. After weeks or months and sometimes even years of physical therapy, he may restore some or all movement of the part of his body that was affected by the stroke. This scenario is just one of myriad situations where we can see and comprehend the reality of the physical body working with and sometimes, as in this example, not complying with the desires of the immaterial mind.

The desires of the human mind are always to move forward towards attaining what we want. It may be the perfect job, perfect wife, perfect husband, perfect home, etc. In moving towards a better life with better things, we use our ever imperfect, decomposing and aging body. If we are lucky enough to attain what it is we want in life, it will not last long, time and our aging body will make sure of that.

This is the same situation between our soul and our spirit as stated above in Chapter 8. Our imperfect soul longs for what is perfect, and we try hard using our imperfect body and imperfect mind/soul to find and attain some sense of perfection, wherever and whenever we can obtain it. We, as humans have a *longing* for 'perfect' things, events, persons or even just moments. I'm sure we can recall 'perfect' encounters we have had in our lives and wish it would last forever. Where does this concept of 'perfection' come from?

We don't want things to end when life is good, and we do not want to exist when life is extremely bad or at least we don't want to exist in an extremely horrible situation for any length of time. Why is it that we are always looking for, or longing for this 'perfect something' out there that must exist, since we are always, if not looking, at least hoping for this 'perfection?' And if we were to find it, what would it be like, feel like or look like?

The Bible uses many words to express the perfection of something or someone, for example the following are words used in the Bible to describe 'perfect'; pure, blameless, mature, and complete. If something is pure, it means that there is absolutely nothing that is intermingled with that substance. If someone is blameless, then that person has done absolutely nothing to which blame, or guilt can be attached. If a person is 'mature,' we understand that they have come to the *full* understanding of what makes that person mature in the very thing they grow into. If something or someone is 'complete' then that thing or person lacks absolutely nothing, everything that makes that thing or person complete is present within the person or thing.

By 'definition' God is; pure, blameless, complete; PERFECT! And since God exists and He is not part of the substance of this world, He must be a transcendental being that exists outside of the realm of space-time and physical matter. *"God is spirit and those who worship Him must worship Him in **spirit** and truth," John 5:24.* Although God is pure spirit and not physical as we know physicality, He does possess a spiritual body, a body that was recognizable by Adam and Eve, which enabled them to see Him and walk with Him. What kind of body God possesses is beyond our imagination, but when we get to heaven we will see Him as He is; *"Beloved, now **we are children of God;** and it has not yet been revealed what we shall be, but we know that when He is revealed, **we shall be like**

*Him, for **we shall see Him as He is**, 1 John 3:2. "Behold He is coming with clouds and every eye **will see Him**, even **they** who pierced Him," Revelation 1:7.*

When God created Adam, He created him; *"of the dust of the ground," and "breathed into his nostrils the breath of **life** and man became a living being," Genesis 2:7.* Adam was both physical matter (atoms and molecules-from the dust of the ground-dead elements-earthly) and spirit substance (a living being). The awakening of Adam's consciousness as well as his body took place when God breathed 'life' into Adam's nostrils and into the rest of his body; "***A body** without the **spirit** is **dead**," James 2:25.*

God's 'breath of life' made the lifeless body of Adam 'alive.' Adam became a living *spirit* with a *conscious soul* capable of knowing and understanding his Creator. The human soul, although immaterial, is extremely complex. The conscious aspect of our soul enables us to know that we can know, or that we are conscious of our consciousness.

The breath of life from God allowed Adam to be alive, to be human with a spirit, soul and body. Adam's consciousness allowed Adam to know God and fully express his thoughts and emotions to God. Remember, a born-again believer possesses; 1.) an un-regenerated body, 2.) a partially sanctified soul and a 3.) perfect spirit. A born-again believer's perfect God-infused spirit has been separated from his soul, *"For the word of God is living and powerful, and sharper than any two-edged sword, piercing even to the **division of soul and spirit"**, Hebrews 4:12,* and removed from the kingdom of darkness and placed in the heavenly realms at the point of conversion. *"He __has delivered__ us from the kingdom of darkness and conveyed us into the kingdom of the Son of His love,"* Colossians 1:13.

The workings of the soul and things done in the body will be judged in heaven, for the purpose of receiving rewards for the things done out of a pure heart for God. The things done out of self-righteous acts to puff ourselves up and benefit ourselves, will be of no heavenly benefit; *"For no other foundation can anyone lay than that which is laid, which is Jesus Christ. Now if anyone builds on this foundation with gold, silver, precious stones, wood, hay, straw, each one's work will become clear; for the Day will declare it, because it will be revealed by fire; and **the fire will test each one's work of what sort it is.** If anyone's work which he has built on it endures, he will receive a **reward. If anyone's work is burned, he will suffer loss; but he himself __will be saved__,** yet as through fire,"* 1 Corinthians 3:11-15.

The 'foundation' stated in the above scripture is the 'foundation' of all creation, or in other words, Jesus Christ. He is the Creator of all creation, *"For **by Him all things were created** that are in heaven and that are on earth, visible and invisible, whether thrones or dominions or principalities or powers. **All things were created through Him** and **for Him**,"* Colossians 1:16.

We as humans can build on this foundation, for that is the purpose of having a foundation. Without a foundation, whatever is built will surely come crashing down. What we cannot do is build our own foundation or our own view of creation that does not line up with the actual creation created by the Creator. Our view of creation or our 'worldview of life' can only be that which ornaments the foundation. A simplistic analogy would be the Christmas tree, whereas the Christmas tree is the foundation of creation (Jesus) and what ornaments we use or how we dress it up is our worldview of that foundation.

The scripture states that we cannot lay another foundation than what has already been laid or to put it another way, there is no other creator of the universe other than Jesus Christ! Building on this reality is allowed and appropriate, however, since what you build is based on your belief system it is imperative that you have the right belief system or the belief system that is founded on the truths of God's word-the Bible, that is the *starting point*.

The scripture mentioned above (1 Corinthians 3:11-15), is clearly talking about a 'born-again' believer's work not a *nonbeliever's* work. This is clearly pointed out at the end of the scripture; *"If anyone's work which he has built on endures, he will receive a reward.* **If anyone's work is burned, he will suffer loss; but he himself <u>will be saved</u>."** So, what does this mean, receiving a reward for works that endure and suffering loss for works that are burned up, for a born-again, saved believer? When and where are believers doing things that will be burned up? Obviously when God receives the work of the believer, that work will be perfect, for it must be perfect, for God to receive it.

When we are moved by the Holy Spirit to do something for God, the work that is done from a pure heart (soul), knowing that God is the impetus for the commencement and completion of that work, is perfect. This perfect work is being accomplished by an imperfect/perfect person-the believer! The believer moves about in an imperfect body, making decisions in the imperfect mind/soul to accomplish a perfect work that has been prompted by the Holy Spirit of God, in the perfect spirit of the believer. As an ex-Marine, this was made evident in battlefield training.

During Bootcamp training a trainee must adhere to the strictest absolute commands of the Drill Sergeant. There is no room for error, for error results in the most dramatic, horrific and painful penalties given by the Drill Instructors. During inspection time, the expectations are heightened to a greater degree. One iota of sloppiness or disorder concerning our bedding, barracks, uniform, posture and even facial expression are met with an iron fist. This is but one of the many obstacles trainees face during the first phase of becoming a Marine.

After successful completion of boot-camp training, one is given the earned title of a 'United States Marine' and sent to Camp Pendleton for Battlefield Training (ITR: Infantry Training Regiment). This is the second phase of becoming a full-fledged Marine. It is during this training phase that the first phase starts to kick in automatically. A Marine who has endured 'Bootcamp,' is now mentally, emotionally and physically fit to be trained for war. This phase of training uses real ammunition and, an 'as real as possible' war scenario, that the Marine may gain some sense of what it will be like in real battle. The interesting thing that took place in this phase, that I personally experienced, is that the 'absolute perfection' in our appearance such as glass polished boots, perfect starched uniforms, etc.... were no longer an issue.

In the middle of 'training for war,' whether it was Battlefield Training (or in real war), the Sergeants and Officers in charge are now concerned with learning what must be done to win the battle, while saving the lives of Marines. The Bible is sort of like this scenario. The Old Testament is what the first phase of Marine Corps training was like in that everything for the Jewish nation was implemented, commanded, inspected and judged by God to the point of death in some situations for not perfectly obeying His commands. The New Testament is somewhat like the second phase of training that pertains to the upkeep of a Marines visual physical attire. No longer is there a concern for the perfection in wearing the uniform because no Marine is concerned with how disheveled, torn or out of order his uniform is, when he is in battle-field training, or in real battle. When the Marine is crawling through mud while being shot at there is no thought of how bad the consequences are going to be over how tattered his uniform is or how muddy his boots are, this should be self-evident.

In a nutshell, before a person became a Marine there was no thought about the dire consequences of being 'out of order' in their attire. In becoming a Marine, that was one of the major concerns that was at the forefront of a Marine's daily thinking, that is, until he is taken out to battle. Everything now changes. What was once not allowed is not only allowed, it is not even important enough to be a small issue, as a matter of fact, it is no issue at all!

The Commanders in charge of military personnel understand the irrational and illogical thought of having their men fight in battle with the idea that if they smudge, tear or soil, in anyway, their uniform while in battle, there will be severe consequences. This is what sin is like, in that, sin in the Old Testament, is likened to a Marine having his uniform out of order, disheveled or torn and tattered when he is *not* in the war zone fighting a battle. When a Marine, however, is in the war zone fighting a battle the regulations concerning his attire are no longer in effect. In a similar manner, this is what it is like for a born-again Christian when it comes to his or her sins. Before becoming a child of God, or a 'true born-again Christian,' that person's body, soul and spirit are steeped in sin. There is no part of that person that does not sin, whether they think they sin or not. Every NON-born-again person is *a sinner* and every TRUE-born-again Christian is *a sinner*. The difference is that one is saved and the other is not. The sins of all born-again Christians, are not held against them, because they have been removed and are continually being removed and never held against him, why? Because he/she is now in the *war zone* and in the *battle!* The battle field now becomes the believer's old self; body and soul/mind (worldview) and Satan and his minions, while the war zone is the world and worldly friends and worldly family.

Before becoming a true born-again Christian, the world was is the sinner's playground, but after becoming a born-again Christian, the world and its worldly system is now the war zone where battles are fought every day. The world now hates you because you are a Christian, and friends and family either, do not want anything to do with you or your "religion," or they tolerate you as long as you don't push your Godly views on them (the very things God wants Christians to do). *"If the world hates you, you know that it hated Me before it hated you. "If you were of the world, the world would love its own. Yet because* **you are not of the world,** *but I chose you out of the world, therefore* **the world hates you**," *John 15:18,19.*

Satan and his minions are also fully against any true born-again believer and will do anything to distract a Christian from doing the will of God. Make no mistake about it, a true born-again, God fearing Christian, is always in the war-zone! God is fully aware of His children's predicament as He is the one who put them there. God knew before he created mankind what He would have to endure to get us saved and what believers would have to endure to walk in His plan of salvation.

It is the *imperfect* soul/mind of a believer that is in the mix of this ungodly world along with his *perfect* spirit that is now filled with God's Holy Spirit and within the perfect spiritual realm of God that makes a believer the perfect-imperfect person! In short, when a person first becomes a child of God, at the point of conversion, their spirit immediately becomes *perfect,* *"For by one offering, He has* **perfected forever**, *those who are* **being sanctified**," *Hebrews 10:14,* but their imperfect soul/mind is in desperate need of renewing, *"And do not be conformed to this world, but be* **transformed** *by* **the renewing of your mind**, *that you may prove what is that good and acceptable and perfect will of God, Romans 12:2.*

It is obvious from the above stated scripture that God wants us to renew our minds, which is at the center of our soul, because one of the most obvious things a believer knows, or should know, is that their mind is not perfect. The believer's mind is always in need of daily renewal.

It is through our perfect born-again God filled spirit that allows the born-again believer to gain and understand spiritual knowledge through the application of God's word (the Bible) and the leading and teaching of the Holy Spirit. An important point needs to be made here about the leading and teaching of the Holy Spirit. The Holy Spirit will never lead or teach someone something that is contrary to God's 'moral will' revealed in scripture. There is no new doctrine that needs to be declared to humanity. God has declared it to us through His word. God has perfectly carried out His plan of salvation using imperfect people to execute his perfect plan of salvation. At whatever age a person becomes born-again, that is the number of years of built up false beliefs and wrong thinking that needs to be renewed through the cleansing of God's word.

I am not stating that everything that a person comes to know prior to being born-again is wrong or false. I am, however, saying that a person's concept of how the visible as well as the invisible-spiritual world works (if they believed in an invisible-spiritual world prior to being born-again), needs to be revisited with the knowledge of God's word, that their mind may be renewed. For example, since the Bible states, *"In the beginning God created the heavens and the earth," Genesis 1:1,* then the obvious conclusion is that the universe was created by a Creator. All that the universe consists of, had a beginning and, therefore, cannot be eternal or infinite. It also means that mankind was created and put on this earth by God Himself with a purpose.

As stated in chapter one of this book, 'you' are His purpose and being an imperfect-perfect being, if you are 'born-again, is part of His plan. God is fully aware of our corrupted, dishonorable and weak natural physical body with its depraved physical and soulful lust for whatever it wants when it wants it.

In God's eye's, every born-again believer is righteous, glorious and destined to eternal life with Him in His heavenly kingdom. This is due only to their *belief* in the gospel message of Christ Jesus. Like a soldier in battle with a tattered and muddied uniform, the unredeemable depraved body and the imperfect soul/mind of the born-again believer has no relevance to their *perfect* standing with God.

In the same manner, true born-again Christians should have no thought about their sins other than the fact, that they have been removed from them and they now have the power to stop sinning! Consider the following scriptures; *"Behold the Lamb of God who **takes away the sins of the world**," John 1:29, "when He had by Himself **purged our sins,** sat down at the right hand of the Majesty on high," Hebrews 1:3. "Therefore He is able to **save to the uttermost** those who come to God through Him, since He always lives to make **intercession for them**," Hebrews 7:25. "And as Moses lifted up the serpent in the wilderness, even so must the Son of Man be lifted up, that **whoever believes in Him should not perish but have eternal life.** For God so loved the world that He gave His only begotten Son that **whoever believes in Him should not perish but have everlasting life,**" John 3:14-16. "Most assuredly, I say to you, he who **hears My word and believes** in **Him** who sent Me **has everlasting life, and shall not** come into judgment, but **has passed from death into life**," John 5:24. "Most assuredly, I say to you, **he who believes in Me has everlasting life**," John 6:47. "As the living Father sent Me, and I live* *because of the Father, so **he who feeds on Me** will live because of Me. "This is the bread which came down from heaven-not as your fathers ate the manna, and are dead. He who eats this bread **will live forever,"** John 6:57-58. "I am the resurrection and the life. He who **believes in Me,** **though he may die, he shall live**. "And whoever lives and **believes in Me** **shall never die**," John 11:25.*

If the born-again believer still believes that the only way to get right with God after committing a sin is by confessing their sins, then this is what he or she is implying; the above eight scriptures are false-Jesus was lying when He stated them, God no longer honors the sacrifice of His Son Jesus because you will take over from here on out, eternal life is no longer eternal because you can lose it if you commit a sin and forgot to confess it, His death on the cross was not quite as complete as the God the Father declares it to be and He, therefore, died in vain since you are the one responsible to make sure you get yourself into heaven by confessing your sins (and you must confess ALL your sins, those committed purposely and those committed in ignorance-how does someone bring to mind sins they don't remember?).

I emphasis 'all' because even in the Old Testament animal sacrifices were made for the "sins committed in ignorance." Remember, without the shedding of blood there is no remission of sins! Whose blood will you shed when you confess your sins? He or she that believes that confessing your sins will get you right with God has made the decision to replace what Christ Jesus did for them on the cross by confessing their own sins (as if somehow that would absolve you from your sins?).

Another point is, if we need to confess our sins to get right with God, then why would we have to confess what He does not want to remember? Jesus paid the ultimate price for His Father *not* to remember our sins any longer! *"For I will be merciful to their **unrighteousness** and their **sins** and **lawless deeds**, I will remember **no more**,"* Hebrews 8:12. As a believer works out the plan of God in this realm, his imperfect soul slowly starts to be perfected and moves towards the perfection of his God filled spirit.

Believers can and do 'perfect' works of God using the imperfect body and imperfect soul, but can only do so, if their spirit has been born of God, which automatically becomes *perfected* when God's Holy Spirit enters the believer's spirit, *"For by one offering, He has **perfected forever**, those who are **being sanctified**,"* Hebrews 10:14.

The authors of the Bible, who were led by Holy Spirit, make it clear that God does not hold their sins against them. Let's take a look at the Book of Hebrews, Chapter 11, known as the *'Hall of Faith'* chapter. There you will find the faithful actions of some of the Old Testament saints that made it on 'God's list of people' worthy enough to be used as an example in the New Testament for us to follow. Some of these people are; Noah, Abraham, Moses, Jacob, Rahab, Samson and King David.

What is extremely interesting about these Old Testament saints depicted in the Book of Hebrews Chapter 11, is the fact that God chose to declare to us *only the good deeds* they did, and left out every evil and despicable thing they did!

There is no mention in the New Testament of Noah's drunken nakedness, *"And Noah began to be a farmer, and he planted a vineyard.*

Then he drank of the wine and was drunk, and became uncovered in his tent. And Ham the father of Canaan, saw the nakedness of his father, and told his two brothers outside, Genesis 9:20-22, or Abraham's deceitfulness, fearfulness and lack of faith in not believing God at His word that he would be the father of many nations through Sarah, *"And Abraham journeyed from there to the South, and dwelt between Kadesh and Shur and stayed in Gerar. Now Abraham said of Sarah his wife, "**She is my sister**." And Abimelech king of Gerar sent and took Sarah. But God came to Abimelech in a dream by night, and said to him, "Indeed you are a dead man because of the woman whom you have taken, for **she is a man's wife**,"* Genesis 20:1-3. *"Then Abimelech said to Abraham, "What did you have in view, that you have done this thing? And Abraham said, "Because I thought, surely the fear of God is not in this place; and **they will kill** me on account of **my wife**,* Genesis 20:10-12.

There is no mention of Moses' refusal to go back to Egypt to confront Pharaoh about setting the children of Israel free after God appeared to him in a 'burning bush, turned a rod into a serpent and back into a rod, turned Moses' hand into a Lepers hand and then back to his normal healthy hand (read Genesis Chapter 3 & 4) and then still complained to God that he did not want to go, *"O my Lord, please send by the hand of **whomever else** You may send." So, the anger of the Lord was kindled against Moses,"* Genesis 4: 13, 14.

Or Jacob's collusion with his mother to deceive his father Isaac to steal his brother's 'first-born blessing,' nor Jacob's blasphemous lie to his father that 'God' was the one who quickly brought him the game he was eating, (read Genesis Chapter 27), *"But Isaac said to his son, "How is it that you have found it so quickly, my son?" "And he said, "Because **the Lord your God brought it to me."** Then Isaac said to Jacob, "Please come near, that I may feel you, my son, whether you are really my son Esau or not." So Jacob went near to Isaac his father, and he felt him and said, "The voice is Jacob's voice, but the hands are the hands of Esau." And he did not recognize him, because his hands were hairy like his brother Esau's hands; so he blessed him. Then he said, "**Are you really my son Esau**?" He said, "**I am**,"* Genesis 27:21-24, or Rahab the HARLOT! *"Now Joshua the son of Nun sent out two men from Acacia Grove to spy secretly, saying "Go, view the land, especially Jericho." So they went, and came to the **house of a harlot** named Rahab, and lodged there,"* Joshua 2:1. *"Now the city shall be doomed by the Lord to destruction, it and all who are in it. Only **Rahab the harlot** shall live, she and all who are with her in the house, because she hid the messengers that we sent,"* Joshua 6:17, or Samson and his sexual relation with a harlot, *"Now Samson went to Gaza and saw a harlot there, and **went in to her**,"* Judges 16:1, and finally King David who lusted for another man's wife and placed her husband in an inescapable position in battle that ensured his death, to have for himself, that man's wife. This one has all the ingredients of; absolute selfishness, lies, lust, betrayal, deceit, cover-up and murder.

*"Then it happened one evening that David arose from his bed and walked on the roof of the king's house. And from the roof he **saw a woman bathing, and woman was very beautiful to behold.***

So David sent and inquired about the woman. And someone said, "Is this not Bathsheba, the daughter of Eliam, the wife of Uriah the Hittite?"

Then David sent messengers, and **took her***; and she came to him, and* **he lay with her***, for she was cleansed from her impurity; and she returned to her house.*

And the woman conceived; so she sent and told David, and said, "I am with child."

Then David sent to Joab, saying, "Send me Uriah the Hittite." And Joab sent Uriah to David.

When Uriah had come to him, David asked how Joab was doing, and how the people were doing, and how the war prospered.

And David said to Uriah. "Go down to your house and wash your feet." So Uriah departed from the king's house, and a gift of food from the king followed him.

But Uriah slept at the door of the king's house with all the servants of his lord, and did not go down to his house.

So when they told David, saying "Uriah did not go down to his house." David said to Uriah, "Did you not come from a journey? Why did you not go down to your house?"

And Uriah said to David, "The ark and Israel and Judah are dwelling in tents, and my lord Joab and the servants of my lord are encamped in the open fields. Shall I then go to my house to eat and drink and to lie with my wife? As you live, and as your soul lives, I will not do this thing," 2 Samuel 11:2-11.

*"In the morning it happened that **David wrote a letter to Joab and sent it by the hand of Uriah.** And he wrote in the letter, saying, "Set Uriah in the forefront of the hottest battle, and **retreat from him, that he may be struck down and die.**" 2 Samuel 11:14.*

"When the wife of Uriah heard that Uriah her husband was dead, she mourned for her husband.

And when her mourning was over, David sent and brought her to his house, and she became his wife and bore him a son. But the thing that David had done displeased the Lord." 2 Samuel 11:26, 27.

These are some of the Old Testament saints whose names are written in the Book of Hebrews being depicted by God as people of faith. However, there is absolutely no mention of their sins, that were clearly written in the Old Testament? Not even one is mentioned! As a matter of fact, they are given quiet a salutation in the Book of Hebrews; *"And what more shall I say? For the time would fail me to tell of Gideon and Barak and Samson and Jephthah, also of David and Samuel and the prophets: who through faith subdued kingdoms, worked righteousness, obtained promises, stopped the mouths of lions, quenched the violence of fire, escaped the edge of the sword, out of weakness were made strong, became valiant in battle, turned to flight, the armies of the aliens…And all these, having obtained a good testimony through faith, did not receive the promise. God having provided something better for us, that they **should not be made perfect apart from us**." Hebrews 11:32-34, 39-40.*

These Old Testament saints cannot be made perfect without us. Why? Because they did not have the infilling of the Holy Spirit in their spirit.

The infilling of the Holy Spirit into a person's spirit is the 'mystery of God' that the next chapter will expound on.

CHAPTER 10

THE MYSTERY

"...the mystery which has been hidden from ages and from generations, but now has been revealed to His saints. To them God will to make know what are the riches of the glory of this mystery among the Gentiles: which is Christ in you, the hope of glory," **Colossians 1:26,27**

When someone talks about gravity or energy we understand what they mean when they use the words 'gravity,' or 'energy,' nevertheless it is still a mystery as to exactly what they are? There are many theories as to what they might be, but no one is certain about what they really are. We build our civilization using the realities of the certainty of the *effects* of these things we call 'gravity' and 'energy.'

Great men of Science and Physics write books about the effects of gravity and energy, but still, it remains a mystery, even though it is a daily experiential phenomenon. In a similar manner, the 'mystery' of God, was such, that it was unknown to man what God really had in mind for the future of mankind here on earth and in His heavenly kingdom. However, unlike the mystery of gravity and energy, God's mystery, concerning His plan for humanity, has been revealed to mankind. God revealed it first to his holy apostles and prophets, to pen His thoughts (the Bible) that, we, like them, would come know the 'things of God' and especially the 'mystery' of God.

The 'mystery' of God answers the questions; 'Why am I here? What is life all about? Where am I going when I die? If we are truly honest about the purpose, meaning and destination of our lives, we find that there is much we do not know about our existence while we travel through time and space on this planet, in this immense universe. Even for the born-again believer, who knows his destination is heaven, the 'how' is still a great mystery and more so, the plan of God for all creation.

There is great comfort in understanding God's plan for us individually and an even greater sense of awe and appreciation in understanding His plan for the whole world. As you will read in this upcoming scripture, the 'mystery kept secret since the world began'; is revealed to the entire world (all nations). *"Now to Him, who is able to establish you according to my gospel and the preaching of Jesus Christ, according to the revelation of the* **mystery kept secret since the world began** *but* **now made manifest,** *and* **by the prophetic Scriptures** *made known to* **all nations,** *according to the commandment of the everlasting God, for obedience to the faith,"* Romans 16:25,26.

The above stated scripture presents us with three important issues, of which the first is, that God had a secret, and second, that this secret was a mystery, and third, He renounced secrecy by revealing this secret to everyone through the prophetic scriptures, otherwise known as the Bible and through the revealing of worldly and universal events as they unfold in time. We can deduce that God revealed it to the authors of the Bible, to pen God's thoughts and will for all mankind. This secret was hidden from everyone including the spirits, principalities and the powers in the heavenly realms. The mystery, in part, remains a mystery even after it's secrecy has been exposed.

Imagine someone telling you that they have a secret and the secret is about a product that is unknown to the world. When that person tells you what the secret is you are still dumbfounded as to what it is and how it even works, even though it is clearly explained and drawn out to you. Think about how many things technology has given to mankind that were once secrets as the inventors worked on their product until it was finished and approved for sale.

Most of us, especially the older generation are still perplexed as to how these tech-toys work, or in other words the secret is no longer a secret, but it is a mystery to us as to how these things operate. The mystery of God's plan also has many facets that we may not immediately understand, as we will soon see. *"To me, who am less than the least of all the saints, this grace was given, that I should preach among the Gentiles the unsearchable riches of Christ, and to make all see what is the **fellowship of the mystery,** which from ages has been **hidden in God** who created all things through Jesus Christ; to the intent that **now** the manifold wisdom of God might be **<u>made known by the church</u> to the principalities and powers in the heavenly places,** according to the eternal purpose which He accomplished in Christ Jesus our Lord, Ephesians 3:8-11.*

All the spiritual beings, who are living in the heavenly realms with God the Father, from the time they were created, were not privy to His secret and to what He was doing with us puny earthlings here on earth. Not until the time of Pentecost when the Holy Spirit first appeared as tongues fire over the heads of the believers in Jerusalem, did they start to understand God's plan for all humanity. *"When the Day of Pentecost had fully come, they were all with one accord in one place. And suddenly there came a sound from heaven, as of **a rushing mighty <u>wind</u>**, and it filled the whole house where they were sitting. Then there appeared to them divided tongues, **as of fire**, and one sat upon each of them,"* Acts 2:3. What is this all about? It is about John 3:1-8; *"Most assuredly, I say to you, unless one is born again he cannot see the kingdom of God. "Most assuredly I say to you, unless one is born of water **and the Spirit**, he cannot enter the kingdom of God. "That which is born of the flesh is flesh and that which is **born of the Spirit is spirit**, "Do not marvel that I said to you, you must be born again.' "The **<u>wind</u> blows** where it wishes, and you hear the sound of it, but **cannot tell where it comes from** and where it goes. So is everyone who is **born of the Spirit."***

Jesus uses the 'wind' and its effect on earth as a parable to illustrate what it is like to be a true born-again believer. God is using the word 'wind' as a synonym for 'person.' The phrase *"A mighty rushing wind"* represents the Holy Spirit and the word 'wind' in *"The wind blows where is wishes,"* represents a born-again believer. We can feel the wind blow in one direction and then in the opposite direction within seconds. So where exactly does the wind come from? We can ask the same of the born-again believer. Where does the born-again believer come from and where is that born-again believer going?

The Bible makes it clear that a born-again believer is NOT from this world or this dimension. What? How does a person, born into this world go from being a human-earthling to becoming an 'alien,' who is no longer of this world?

This sounds like nonsense and to the natural mind, yes, this is nonsense, however, not to the person who is 'born-again,' and 'no longer of this world.' If you are a born-again believer, whether you have ever thought about it or not, you are **no longer of this world**, "*I have given them Your word; and the world has hated them because* **they are not of the world,** *just as I am not of the world I do not pray that You should take them out of the world, but that You should keep them from the evil one. They are* **not of the world,** *just as* **I am not of the world,**" "*I do not pray for these alone, but* **also for those who will believe in Me through their word;** *that they all may be one, as* **You, Father, are in Me,** *and* **I in You;** *that* **they also may be one in Us,**" *John 17:14-16, 20,21.*

God's secret, although it has been revealed to us in His word, is still a mystery and much of it will remain a mystery until we are called home to be with Him, at which point we will know all about the total plan of God, with no mysteries left to learn. Until now, we can come to know much of the mysteries of God and by 'faith' believe, what might seem to be impossibilities imbedded in His mysteries.

One of the great mysteries in the Bible is the fact that God the Father, Jesus Christ and the Holy Spirit are one and the same God - the Holy

Trinity. How can three persons be one God? The 'how' is a mystery, the fact that they 'are one' is not. The intellect will remain befuddled with that mystery, however, believing by faith, and through the studying of God's word, a person can conclude that God is a Triune God.

The creation of the entire universe is a mystery, who created it, is not. How Jesus brought the universe into creation is a mystery, the fact that He brought it into creation is not. *"**All things** were **made through Him**, and without Him nothing was made that was made…He was in the world, and **the world was made through Him**, John 1:3,10. "He is the image of the invisible God, the firstborn over all creation. For **by Him all things were created** that are in heaven and that are on earth, visible and invisible, whether thrones or dominions or principalities or powers. **All things were created through Him** and for Him," Colossians 1:15,16.*

God has revealed His secret and His mystery to mankind. It is His will that His mysterious plan, develop and come to fruition before the eyes of the principalities and powers in the heavenly realms. This grand event, when God began to pour out His Holy Spirit into the spirit of men and women was a 'mystery,' but now it is neither a secret not a mystery. *"…the mystery which has been hidden from ages and from generations, but now has been revealed to His saints. To them God willed to make known what are the riches of the glory of this mystery among Gentiles: which is **Christ in you** the hope of glory, Colossians 1:26, 27. "…having made known to us the **mystery of His will,** according to His good pleasure which He purposed in Himself, that in the dispensation of the fullness of the times He* *might **gather together in one all things in Christ**, both which are in heaven and which are on earth-in Him, Ephesians 1:9,10.*

This 'mystery' that the Bible talks about has several components to it; *"For this reason I, Paul, the prisoner of Christ Jesus for you Gentiles–if indeed you have heard of the dispensation of the grace of God which was given to me for you, how that by revelation He made known to me **the mystery** (as I have briefly written already, by which, when you read, you may understand my knowledge in the **mystery of Christ**), which in other ages **was not made known to the sons of men**, as it has now been revealed by the Spirit to His holy prophets: that **the Gentiles should be fellow heirs, of the same body, and partakers of His promise in Christ through the gospel**, Ephesians 3:1-7.*

Clearly one of the components of God's mystery is the Gentiles partaking of God's promises that He promised to the nation of Israel, *"For I do not desire, brethren, that you should be ignorant of this **mystery**, lest you should be wise in your own opinion, that blindness in part has happened to Israel until **the fullness of the Gentiles has come in**, Romans 11:25.* It is no longer a secret that the Gentiles will partake of God's new covenant along with the Jews.

Scripture is very clear about; the what, the how, the why, the when and the where, of the new covenant between God and those who choose to partake of the new covenant Why then is it a mystery? It is a mystery because as the Bible states, God's ways are not man's ways and God's thoughts are not man's thoughts, *"For My thoughts are not your thoughts, nor are your ways My ways, say the Lord. For as the heavens are higher than the earth, so are My ways higher than your ways and My thoughts than your thoughts," Isaiah 55:8,9.*

What God has done is made two separate people, the Jews and the Gentiles, 'ONE.' In other words, there is no longer, in the New Testament time that we are living in, right at this moment, Jew or Gentile. *"There is neither Jew nor Greek, there is neither slave nor free, there is neither male, nor female; for you are **all one _in_ Christ** Jesus," Galatians 3:28.*

'How' God will accomplish what He set out to accomplish is a mystery, but the fact that He is accomplishing His plan is not a mystery. How God 'makes us sit in heavenly places,' while we are still in this world is a mystery, but the fact that born-again believers 'sit in heavenly places in Christ Jesus' is not mystery. It is a fact given to us in His holy word. *"...and raised us up together, and **made us sit together in heavenly places** in Christ Jesus," Ephesians 2:6. "**I will** put My laws into **their minds**, and **I will** write them upon **their hearts**. And I will be their God...For **I will** be merciful to their iniquities and **I will remember their sins no more."** Hebrews 8:10, 12.*

'How' God puts His laws into our mind and writes them on our hearts is a mystery, but the fact that He does it, is not a mystery, for with God all things are possible (Mark 10:27). *"For by one offering **He** has **perfected forever** those that are **being sanctified,"** Hebrews 10:14. "**Whoever is born of God does not sin**; for His seed remains in him: and he **cannot sin** because he is **born of God,"** 1 John 3:9-10.*

The truth of God's word, depicted in the scriptural passages above, are of utmost importance in understanding the solution to our 'ever sinning' problem. We can't help but sin in word, thought or deed and yet, God's word tells us that we "cannot" sin? God is a holy God and will not reside with sin, therefore, we need to be 'sinless' to go to heaven AND, we do not have the ability to annihilate sin from our life while we live in this physical body within the confines of this physical universe.

The solution, then, is obvious, we just need to become sinless, but not only sinless, we must also take on a 'different nature' if we are to exist in a totally and completely 'different in nature,' immaterial dimension that is not in the least similar, to the dimension we currently live in, or in other words, a dimension where physical matter, as we know it to be, does not exist.

The problem deepens for us, because we not only do not have the inclination nor the moral fortitude to become what God requires us to become, we also, do not have the intellect to know *how to be sinless*, nor do we have the resources or power to change our sinful nature. Thank God, that, we, however, are not left hopeless nor helpless. The solution is not ours to create nor to implement. Our is only to humbly receive the solution, and in doing so we become a *'new creation'* by being transformed into a 'new creature' of a 'different nature.' Becoming a *'new creation'* of a *'different nature'* is part of the mystery of God. This new creation is something that not even God's Angels were aware of. The interesting thing about being a 'new creation' is that you cannot know or fully understand the concept of being a 'new creation' until you 'actually become' a 'new creation.'

While living here in this physical realm, the *'new creation'* has an unredeemable earthly body, a work in progress soul and a perfect God filled spirit. If we are born-again, we are no longer of this world, *"I have given them Your word; and the world has hated them because **they are not of the world,** just as I am not of the world I do not pray that You should take them out of the world, but that You should keep them from the evil one. They are **not of the world,** just as **I am not of the world,"** "I do not pray for these alone, but **also for those who will believe in Me through their word;** that they all may be one, as You, Father, are in Me, and I in You; that **they also may be one in Us,"** John 17:14-16, 20,21.*

The moment we received Jesus as Lord and Savior, we gave up our worldly citizenship and our worldly identity. If we are male, we are no longer male, if we are female we are no longer female, if we are Jewish, we are no longer Jewish, if we are Gentile, we are no longer Gentile, *"There is **neither Jew nor Greek,** there is **neither slave or free,** there is **neither male nor female;** for you are all one in Christ Jesus," Galatians 3: 28,29.*

Not being what you experience, as you, being you, is without a doubt, a mystery, however, it is a Biblical fact that you are not what you experience yourself to be. Once you are 'born of the Spirit,' your *spirit,* that you cannot see, touch or feel, is who you really are; the 'mystery of God,' a 'new creation,' 'not of this world'! If this sounds strange, think about the fact that your life is hidden in Christ Jesus, that you (if you are a believer), at this moment are sitting with Him in the heavenly realms, *"even when we were dead through our trespasses, made us alive together with Christ (by grace have ye been saved), and raised us up with Him, and **made us to sit***

with Him in the heavenly places, in Christ Jesus," *Ephesians 2:5-7 (ASV)*. If you are saved, you also have the mind of Jesus Christ; *"But we have the mind of Christ," 1 Corinthians 2:16.*

We know that we cannot read another person's mind, much less have their mind? So how can we have the mind of Christ? Remember that the Father, Son and Holy Spirit are 'ONE,' and since He poured out His Holy Spirit into our spirit, His mind comes with the package. It needs to, because what good is the Spirit of God living in us if there is no mind of God. This is a must, if we are to think the things and the ways of God. Another way to look at this is to understand that God is infinite in every possible way, which means He can fully fill us with His Spirit and never lose from Himself, what He is filling us with, no matter how many people get saved.

We know that the Holy Spirit has a mind, for the Holy Spirit, speaks, teaches, leads, comforts, and convicts (not condemns) us, therefore, this mind of God is in the born-again believer, this is a mystery as to how this operates, but the fact that this is so, is not a mystery because God has revealed it to us in His word, as stated above. What is housed in the mind of God's Holy Spirit is 'truth,' ALL truth! Everything in this universe comes from, and is, sustained by God.

The laws of Nature, the astronomical, biological, psychological, mathematical, physical, etc., processes and entities, were created by God. There is nothing that exist that was not created by Him. He also created us as a three part being; body, soul and spirit. The physical body will always be earthly and will never be redeemed or regenerated. The soul (mind, freewill, desires, emotions, reasoning) is the medium God chose to create us with, that would give us the capability of making a mindful freewill choice to receive or reject the gospel of Christ. It is the spirit of man that God uses for us to be born-again and become a 'new creation' through the indwelling of His Holy Spirit coming into our spirit at the point of receiving Christ as Lord and Savior; this was a secret and a mystery that has now been revealed.

Believing and trusting in Christ as Lord and Savior makes a person's spirit completely new, reborn or born-again, holy, sanctified, complete, perfect, a 'NEW CREATION.' This makes it possible for God the Father, Jesus the Son and the Holy Spirit to make *our spirit* His home, the 'Holy of Holies' where God will reside, a place of absolute perfection created by God, *"For by one offering He has **perfected forever** those who are **being sanctified**," Hebrews 10:14. "I will pray the Father, and He will give you another Helper, that He may **abide with you forever** – the **Spirit of truth**, whom the world cannot receive, because it neither sees Him nor knows Him, but you know Him, for He dwells with you and **will be in you**," John 14: 16,17.* This is a component of the 'mystery of God,' which is God living in our spirit. Only by having the Spirit of God living within our spirit can we cultivate a sincere desire to be more Christ like that we may overcome the desires of the flesh and the powers of this world.

This is the struggle that the great apostle Paul personally went through. He was completely aware of the fact that his body was unredeemable, sinful and totally depraved, *"**But I discipline my body and bring it into subjection**, lest when I have preached to others, I myself* *should become disqualified," 1 Corinthians 9:27.* The Apostle Paul is not talking about being disqualified from his eternal salvation, but rather as a preacher of the word of God. He knows that our body wants what it wants, when it wants it and it is his duty to put his body under disciplinary rule, if he is to overcome the lusts of the flesh. Our bodies were designed this way, to survive, in this physical, material world.

A body that does not get hungry or feel pain will not get the nutrition it needs, which could lead to disastrous health issues. A body that feels no pain could bleed to death through an undetected serious laceration. If our bodies did not feel sexual compulsions, there would be no procreation as God commanded Adam and Eve to do; *"So God created man in His own image; in the image of God He created him; male and female He created them. Then God blessed them, and God said to them, "Be fruitful and multiply; fill the earth and subdue it," Genesis 1:27, 28.*

Unfortunately, even though our unredeemable body, at times, craves for, that which is comforting and healthful, it also wants whatever is sinful and unhealthy and usually in large quantities and for as long as it can attain it. Our soul, however, is redeemable as is our spirit, and can undergo transformation through the sanctification process by the Holy Spirit living in our spirit.

The believer's duty towards sanctification is one of surrender to the workings of the Holy Spirit. *"If I do not wash you, **you** have **no part with Me,**" John 13:8. "He who has **begun a good work in you** will **complete it until the day of Christ Jesus,"** Philippians 1:6.* Our spirit, that is infused with God's Holy Spirit, is instantly illuminated, filled with His presence, sanctified, holy, perfect and righteous upon believing and trusting in Christ. This is because God will not and cannot dwell where sin exists. Jesus experienced this reality on the cross when He purposely took upon Himself the sins of the world; *"Behold the Lamb of God who **takes away the sin of the world**,"* John 1:29. *"Once at the end of the ages, He has appeared to **put away sin** by the sacrifice of Himself,* Hebrews 9:26. *"And at the ninth hour Jesus cried out with a loud voice, saying, "Eloi, Eloi, lama sabachthani?,"* which is translated, *"My God, My God, **why has thou forsaken Me**,"* Mark 15:34.

Jesus paid the penalty for the sin of the world, which is total separation from God, for God cannot and will not dwell with sin. If God the Father separated Himself from His one and only Son, when Jesus took on the sins of mankind to remove our sin and place it upon Himself, why would anyone think that God would hang out with our continually sinful soul?

Separation from God is hell; the absolute finality of inconsolable, darkness, suffering, anguish, horror, etc., for all eternity. God the Father had to reject Jesus because of the depravities of the human-race that were placed upon Him (He became sin willingly), that you and I be set free from the power, the presence and the penalty of sin. *"There is therefore, now no condemnation for those who are **in** Christ Jesus,"* Romans 8:1. For if you are **in** Christ Jesus, He is **in** you! *"If you love Me, keep My commandments. "And I will pray the Father, and He will give you another Helper, that He may **abide with you forever** - "the Spirit of truth, whom the world cannot receive, because it neither sees Him nor knows Him; but you know Him, for He dwells with you and **will be in you**,"* John 14:15-17. **"He** *who did not spare His own Son, but delivered Him up for us all, how shall He not with Him also freely give us all things,"* Romans 8:32.

Born-again believers are a product of the 'mystery of God,' because it was for this purpose that the Son of Man, the Son of God, Jesus the Christ, God incarnate, created all that exists, whether it be visible or invisible, gave Himself up to die a horrific death, that the mystery of God would be manifest in humanity. The 'mystery of God' is "Christ IN you and you in Christ!" This universe and all that is in it, was created with you in mind.

God created the natural world knowing that He would partake of its physical material nature in the body of Christ. He took upon Himself the very likeness of humanity, putting on a body of flesh to allow humanity to tear it up and put to death. This He allowed after repeatedly demonstrating His love for all mankind by the wondrous miracles He worked for all to see.

The dead Christ hanging on the cross gives humanity two distinct profound truths; the hateful, depraved, wicked, godless and corrupt mind of mankind and the righteous, holy, and pure love of God coming together to show us that God loves us and loved us even while humanity nailed Him to the cross. There was no other way to demonstrate to us, just how much He loves us other than to allow mankind to kill Him, Him who had the power to annihilate us with just the breath of his word, at any time, while He was going through the crucifixion process.

What person allows his enemy to kill him in such a horrific manner just to demonstrate to his enemy, his love for him? Those two truths met at the cross of Christ. God demonstrated to us His infinite love towards the very people he created, lived with, cared for and healed, He also demonstrated to us how humanity would react towards His perfect love towards humanity. This in part is a 'mystery.' Why would He do such a thing? Why would He put Himself in such a horrific situation? Why would God knowingly allow humanity, like mad dogs pouncing on their prey, to kill Him with such vicious hatred and impunity? This is where the mystery starts to unveil itself. We know that the Bible states that without the shedding of blood there is no remission of sins, so why not just continue with the sacrificing of the blood of bulls and goats, after all that's what God accepted for centuries? The reason is given to us in His word; *"For the law, having a shadow of the **good things to come**, and not the very image of the things, can **never** with these same sacrifices, which they offer continually year by year, **make those who approach perfect.** For then would they not have ceased to be offered? For the worshipers, once purified, would have had <u>no more consciousness of sins</u>. **But in those sacrifices, there is a <u>reminder of sins every year</u>. For it is impossible that the blood of bulls and goats could take away sins,"** Hebrews 10:1-4.*

It is obvious in the above scripture that: 1.) the law is only a "shadow of the good things to come" (Jesus-the exact image of God), 2.) God demands perfection before one can come to Him, 3.) He does not want us, nor Himself, to remember our sins and 4.) the blood of animals cannot take away our sins.

Who could possibly fit the bill to accomplish perfection for those who come near to Him without the aid of the law to render our conscience clean from sin, with blood, but not with the blood of animals? It would have to be a person and not an animal, someone whose life and blood was sinless, and not just sinless, but someone who could not only touch our heart, but come into the very core of our essence - our immaterial spirit, that we might be cleansed from **all** sin through the power of God's Holy Spirit *living in our spirit*! The obvious answer is Jesus Christ!!

So how is it that our conscience is cleansed from all unrighteousness? Our 'conscience' is another name for our 'moral compass.' It is that part of our consciousness that knows the difference between right and wrong. For a person's conscience to be cleansed of all sin, that person must first have the knowledge that this is possible, second, that person must have the Spirit of God living within their spirit to be able to think the thoughts of God. Thinking the thoughts of God is not some creative, esoteric or metaphoric endeavor, rather the concept of thinking the thoughts of God is quite simple. All one has to do, is read and study His holy word.

In the Bible are the thoughts of God, penned by men who were moved by God's Holy Spirit. His holy word are His thoughts expressed to all humanity. His word (thoughts) tells us that; the believer's sins are no longer held against them, their sins have been removed for all eternity, God Himself, does not want to remember their sins and that the believer has the mind of Christ. Having the mind of Christ is essential if one is to understand, spiritually, the thoughts of God.

When a person comes to 'know' something, the act of knowing is a conscious act that allows that person to respond to that specific knowledge that has been acquired. So, consciously 'knowing' that your conscience is cleansed from all sin is the first step in understanding that whatever sin you commit, is never held against you, or in other words, the sin does not stick to your conscience because you now have the power of God's Holy Spirit living inside your spirit, to walk away from that sin knowing that that sin is not remembered by God, and therefore, not held against you, due to the fact that Jesus paid the penalty for all your sins.

Once you realize that you have committed a sin, the Biblical response would be thanking God, that because of what Jesus has done, that sin that was just committed by you is not held against you; *"My little children, these things I write to you, so that you may not sin. **And if anyone sins, we have an Advocate with the Father, Jesus the righteous,"*** 1 John 2: 1. This scripture is God's thought telling us that, if and, when we sin, God the Father has already taken care of all the issues pertaining to 'sin' through the death of His Son, Jesus. The presence of Jesus Christ sitting at the right hand of the Father is another way of saying 'we have an Advocate with the Father.'

When a 'born-again believer sins,' he or she should not spend time anguishing over their sin or find some way of punishing themselves, instead they should immediately give thanks to Jesus for paying the price for the sin they just committed, while giving thanks to God the Father for not holding that sin against them. Immediately after giving thanks for what Jesus has done for the believer who sinned; the knowledge of the *reality of the removal of the 'penalty'* for that sin should clear their *conscience*. The 'conscience' is that part of the mind/soul that knows right from wrong-our, our moral compass. This knowledge of the *reality of the removal of the penalty of sin* acknowledges that they still stand righteous before God the Father, because of what Jesus accomplished on the cross two-thousand years ago. That sin will still be part of our memory, which is that part of our consciousness/awareness, that remembers the events we do throughout our lifetime. Being conscious is being awake and aware of our surroundings, while being conscientious (using our conscience) is knowing right from wrong, two totally different concepts. It is our *conscience* that is being cleared or in other words deemed 'not-guilty,' by the personal blood sacrifice of Jesus Christ. It is like a Judge declaring that you are 'not-guilty,' by the fact that someone else took the blame for your wrong-doing and you no longer need to bear the burden of guilt.

Our memory, which is seated within our consciousness (not conscience) still remembers the sin, but God's word tells us that we need not hang on to the memory, nor feel condemned. That part of our mind that houses our memory will still remember the sin, however, our conscience or our moral compass, that knows the difference between right and wrong, knows that in God's eyes we are still righteous in His sight, not because of anything we have done or said after sinning, but rather, because of His Son Jesus who is sitting at His right hand, marked with the marks of His crucifixion, paid the penalty of ALL committed sins.

'How' God cleanses our conscience from all sin is a mystery, the fact that He can do it, is not, for with God, all things are possible! When He enters our spirit, we become a 'new creation,' *"Therefore, if anyone is **in Christ**, he is a **new creation**; old things have passed away; behold, **all things** have become new,"* 2 Corinthians 5:17. This my friends, is a mystery. If you are a born-again believer, just look in the mirror. You look the same, so how could you be a 'new creation'? however, not only are you a 'new creation,' ALL things have become new, yet we do not see it. God, however, sees everything from every possible angle. Since He does not live within the continuum of time and space, He can see the beginning and the end of all things.

If you are a born-again believer, He sees you IN Jesus and He sees Jesus IN you – the 'new creation.' He does not see any of your sins or faults, for He chooses not to see nor remember your sins, *"For I will be merciful to their unrighteousness, and their sins and their lawless deeds, I will remember no more," Hebrew 8:12. "There sins and their lawless deeds, I will **remember no more**," Hebrews 10:17.*

God clearly demonstrated this reality of *not remembering* our sins in the book of Hebrews, chapter 11, where the Old Testament saints are recorded as 'heroes of faith.' These Old Testament saints committed some of the most despicable sins and yet there is no mention of their sin(s) in the very chapter that they are being commended for their faith. God could have chosen to include their sins along with their righteous faith, God, however, chose not to do this. Why? God wants nothing to do with sin, which means He does not desire to see it or remember it. His word declares to us that born-again believers sit in the heavenly realms with Him in Christ Jesus! This is because God sees all believers in the heavenly realms, right now, – in spirit! That means every true born-again believer is secured in His plan of salvation; *"My sheep hear my voice and I know them, and they follow Me. "And **I give them eternal life** and they shall **never perish;** <u>neither</u>*

*shall **anyone snatch them out of My hand**.* "*My Father who has given them to Me, is greater than all; and **no one is able to snatch them out of My Father's hand**. "I and My Father are one," John 10:27-30.* When God talks about the born-again believer's salvation status, He uses the present-tense, not the future tense, which means, it's a done deal and that is just the way it is. With God, there are no mistakes. As stated earlier in this chapter; "*There is neither Jew nor Greek, there is neither slave nor free, there is neither male, nor female; for you are **all one in Christ** Jesus," Galatians 3:28.*

When I look in the mirror, I'm still a male Gentile, but God says I am not! When I look in the mirror I am still here on earth, but God says I am not. I am a 'new creation' of God, with the mind of Christ, sitting in heavenly places in Christ Jesus – this was a mysterious secret of God, that is no longer a secret, but remains a mystery as to how this is so. So, what we have now is God's holy word in scripture declaring to us the reality of God's plan for each person and for the whole of humanity.

We have the evidence of nature, the evidence of scripture and the witness of the Holy Spirit within our spirit that allows faith, the size of a mustard seed, to grow into full maturity in the knowledge of our Lord and Savior. That my friends, is not a mystery, but a reality that can easily be accomplished through the reading of scripture, the leading of God's Holy Spirit and the desire to be more Christ like. 'How,' we become more Christ like, is a mystery, but the fact that we can be more Christ like is not, for His word declares that we can become 'Christ-like,' until the completion of all things when we will clearly be as He is, perfect in every way.

CHAPTER 11

THE GIFT

*"If you knew the __gift__ of God, and who it is who says to you, 'Give Me a drink,' you would have **asked Him** and He would have **given you** living water," John 4:10.*

Have you ever received a gift from someone or given a gift to someone? If you have been on the receiving end of an undeserved or unsolicited gift, then you know it can be quiet an event, and I am not talking about receiving a gift because it is your birthday or Christmas or another special event. No, I am talking about a gift that was given to you for no apparent reason other than the person giving you the gift, had you in mind.

If you are like most people you probably would be completely shocked, elated, and surprised, maybe even a little confused. When the feelings of happiness have worn out, there might even be some feelings of guilt on your part to the point that you start thinking about what you are now obligated to give that person now that they have given you a gift. Well, God has given you, personally, as well as the whole human race, a totally and absolutely 'free gift.'

This gift is not like any other gift that a person can give or receive, first of all, because this gift is not from this world. This Gift is from another dimension, and not only is it from another dimension, this gift happens to be the Creator of all visible and invisible creation. Yes, the gift is a person!

God the Father has given us His one and only begotten Son, the *Creator of all creation!* "*He is the image of the invisible God, the firstborn over all creation. For by Him all things were created that are in heaven and that are on earth, visible and invisible, whether thrones or dominions or principalities or powers. All things were created through Him and for Him. And He is before all things, and in Him all things consist,*" *Colossians 1:15-17.* So, not only is the Gift different in its origin and substance, the Gift is also not wrapped up all pretty with a bow or dressed in fine clothes, in the same manner that we wrap up or dress up a gift before handing it or presenting it to the recipient.

This Gift comes from poverty-stricken streets, beaten and torn, bloodied and whipped, punctured and stabbed, dripping in blood and unrecognizable in form. If we were to open a large box that was all wrapped up in beautiful wrapping paper with a large bow and upon opening the box found a bloodied, beaten beyond recognition dead man in the box, my guess is that one would think a great horrific cruel hoax, by some mafia organization, has just played a trick on them. A hoax He is not, rather He is what, God the Father, says He is – a Gift! This Gift was given to all humanity.

There is no one from the time of Adam and Eve that has not been given this gift. *Therefore, as through one man's offense Judgment came to all men, resulting in condemnation, even so through one Man's righteous act the free gift came to ALL MEN, resulting in justification,*" Romans *5:18.* Even the people from the Old Testament, who had no idea of who Jesus was, were also given this gift; "*For Christ also suffered once for sins, the just for the unjust, that He might bring us to God, being put to death in the flesh but made alive by the Spirit, by whom also,* **He went and preached to the spirits in prison**, *who formerly were disobedient, when once the Divine longsuffering waited in the days of Noah, while the ark was being prepared, in which a few, that is, eight souls, were saved through water," 1 Peter 3:18-20.*

These *"spirits in prison,"* are the people, who after physical death, from the time of Adam and Eve up to the time Jesus' death, were held in a spiritual prison (in the same manner as we are held in a physical prison in this physical world in a physical body), that they would have the same chance as those in the New Testament times (now!), to hear and receive or reject the gospel message of Christ Jesus, and Jesus Himself.

This event took place after his death on the cross and prior to the resurrection within the spiritual realm. Imagine yourself, having left this physical world and finding yourself in the spiritual realm knowing that your physical death did not terminate or annihilate your life. Imagine you knowing that you are in the spiritual realm and imprisoned awaiting the penalties and consequences for the sins you committed while alive on earth in your physical body.

Imagine experiencing your soul/consciousness and spirit imprisoned and you cannot cause yourself to cease to exist or exist somewhere else – you have absolutely no control over your existence and you know you are guilty for the sins you have committed. You know that you have no physical body that you can destroy to get out of your predicament and you know that you are in a 'life after physical death' situation with no control over your circumstances! We can only speculate what this spiritual world looked like when Jesus walked into that spiritual realm.

The number of people from Adam until the death of Christ is unknown, but I think it is fair to surmise that the number of people is one of great magnitude. It is important to grasp the idea that when Jesus went into the spiritual realm to preach to the 'spirits in prison,' He was seen, as just another person who had died and is now a disembodied spirit like them and was also imprisoned with them.

After Jesus preached the gospel message to them, they had a choice to believe and accept Him as their Lord and Savior or reject Him (now where have we heard that story before?). Those that chose to believe in Him, he led up into the heavenly realms to spend eternity in their heavenly home. Those that rejected Him probably saw Jesus and those that believed in Him, leave the spiritual prison that they themselves could not get out of, at which point, they had no other recourse than to suffer the consequences of their decision to reject the 'Gift of God.' They have already been through the death of the body and are now existing without a body in the spiritual realm. They will from now on, for all eternity, live in the spiritual realm, but not in heaven.

Those who chose to believe Jesus as to who He said He was, were taken with Jesus into the heavenly kingdom and those who did not, are at this moment, awaiting Judgment Day and their placement into spiritual darkness for all eternity! This is the same story about Jesus in the New Testament while He walked on earth. Jesus came into this world through the birthing process just like any other child. The conception was miraculous and "Spiritual," but the birthing or the coming into the world was normal. To the rest of the world, Jesus was just another person walking on the face of this earth. In the same manner, to the rest of the souls in the spirit world in prison, Jesus was just another spirit. Why should they believe He was who He said He was?

When Jesus said, *"Most assuredly, I say to you, unless one is born of* **water** _and_ **the Spirit**, *he cannot enter the kingdom of God. That which is* **born of flesh is flesh**, *and that which is* **born of Spirit is spirit**," *John 3:5,6.*

He is alluding to the fact that there are only two kinds of people; those in the flesh (unsaved) and those in the Spirit (saved). Jesus is also stating that a person must first be born (flesh) into this physical world first before their spirit can be born again of the Spirit and allowed to enter the kingdom of God. The words 'water' and 'flesh' mean the birthing of a child into this world from the womb of the mother.

The words '*Spirit*' and '_spirit_' mean the Holy *Spirit* entering the _spirit_ of a person when that person believes in Jesus Christ as their Lord and Savior. This also ensures that no fallen angel can make it back into the kingdom of God, why? Angels are spiritual created beings and they are not born of water or in other words, they were not birthed from a mother's water filled, womb. Even if angels were to repent, they could not make it back into God's heavenly kingdom because fallen angels were once in the presence of almighty God; the Father, the Son and the Holy Spirit. They have always known the existence of the Son of God, because from the moment they became conscious angelic-beings they were in the Trinity's presence.

Remember that Jesus stated over and over in the New Testament that whoever 'believes' in Him has eternal life. Well, obviously the fallen angels believe that Jesus is the Son of God, however, their belief is not based on faith, it is based on fact. They know He exists because they lived with Him face to face in the heavenly realms before their fall. On the day they were created, they became conscious-beings looking at the very presence of God – no faith is needed there.

When entering this world as humans, we become conscious of only the physical world around us. It is only after hearing the gospel message of Christ and choosing, by faith, to believe on Jesus that our spirit is born-again into a world not of this dimension. In the spiritual realm, the spirits in prison were not 'born-again.' How could they be? Jesus had not even been born and therefore, there was no sacrifice that could bring eternal life.

All the lambs, goats, bulls, etc., were nothing but reminders of the sins that God's chosen people committed prior to the birth of Christ. Those sacrifices could do nothing to renew their minds much less their spirit. Only through the infilling of God's Holy Spirit is one given entrance into the kingdom of God.

The 'spirits in prison' had to make the decision (non-physical; soul/mind/consciousness), like anyone else, to believe in Jesus as to whom He proclaimed Himself to be, or reject Him, the choice was theirs to make. If they believed in Him, by faith, then their 'dead to God' *spirits* were 'born-again' unto salvation, *"Most assuredly, I say to you, unless one is **born again**, he cannot see the kingdom of God,"* John 3:3.

I don't know about you, but I think that a chance of getting into heaven *after* leaving this physical world and realizing that you continue to live on in the spiritual realm, is a gift! The Old Testament era people had no Messiah, there was no Son of God, who sacrificed His life for the removal of sins. That is why Jesus had to go into the spiritual realm and preach to them.

Today we are living in the New Testament era, the Messiah has come and has sacrificed his life. That means we do not get another chance after we leave this physical world. When we die we will not be in a spiritual realm waiting for a Messiah, for Jesus and His gospel message has been around for over two-thousand years!

During His ministry on this physical earth, Jesus proclaimed; that He and the Father were one and the same, that He was not of this world, that apart from Him no one could do anything, that salvation and entrance into the kingdom of God could only be through Him, and that He was the "gift" of God for all mankind! He raised people from the dead, fed thousands with a few loaves of bread and fish (with more food left over than what He started with) and more people disbelieved rather than believed He was who He said He was.

I believe Jesus preached to the spirits in prison just as he preached to the lost and imprisoned here on earth. Some believed, others did not! As stated earlier in this book, God has removed every obstacle and barrier that could impede the entrance into his heavenly kingdom for everyone, every person ever born into this physical world. He has left only one command – choose life - Jesus! The spirits in prison could not come back into this physical realm to right their wrongs, they could only either believe in Jesus as Lord or reject Him.

Remember the 'thief' who was stuck hanging on the cross? He was physically and hopelessly restrained (physically imprisoned) from accomplishing anything godly or righteous that could get him into the kingdom of heaven. The *"spirits in prison,"* were in the same predicament as the thief hanging on the cross. They were 'imprisoned' and had no way of escaping, no way of coming back to this physical realm to make amends, go to church, give to the poor, etc.

The 'Gift of God' going into the spiritual realm to preach to the spirits in prison demonstrates the mercy, grace and love of God for all humanity. The sins of the *world*, from the time of Adam until the return of Christ, have been 'taken away,' 'paid for,' 'removed,' and are no longer the reason a person will not get into God's heavenly kingdom and they are not the reason someone will be damned to hell for all eternity.

In this physical world that we live in, sin carries with it a *penalty of death*. This death sentence for all mankind is not the dying of the physical body that is laid to rest in the grave, but rather the total and absolute separation from God *for all eternity,* that my friend is death! This penalty, like all other penalties, needs to be accounted for, meted out, atoned for or paid for, however, the problem is that the penalty incurred is incurred at the time of our birth into this physical world.

We are born into this sinful, physical world as a sinful person or in other words, as a human being in a physical body with a soul and spirit *dead to God,* that is why we are sinful, it is our nature to be sinful in a sinful body, in a natural sinful environment. No one born into this world is born perfect into this world, and then, as life progresses, they become sinful. Instead, we are born sinful into this sinful world and progressively do the things of this world-sin, both purposely and in ignorance because of our "dead to God" nature.

If everyone is born dead to God, then there is no person or no 'thing' in this *natural world* that we can use to make us *perfect,* which is what is needed for anyone to get into heaven. Anything we have to offer for our sins is already tainted with sin, or in other words, whatever we try to offer God is of *this world,* and anything of this world is sinful by its natural existence. It is like trying to use mud to cleanse yourself from mud. The only thing that can be used to pay for and cleanse us from our sins is something that is *sinless* AND *not of this world!*

*"So the Jews said, Will He kill Himself, because He says, 'Where I go you cannot come'? And He said to them, "You are from beneath; **I am from above.** You are of this world; **I am not of this world,"** John 8:23."...how much more shall the blood of Christ, who through the eternal Spirit offered Himself **without** spot to God, **cleanse your conscience from dead works** to serve the living God," Hebrews 9:14.*

*"The next day John saw Jesus coming toward him, and said, "Behold! The Lamb of God who **takes away the sin** of the world!" John 1:29.*

"…but now, once at the end of the ages, He has appeared to **put away sin** *by the* **sacrifice of Himself.** *And as it is appointed for men to die once, but after this the judgment, so Christ was* **offered once to bear the sins of many.***" Hebrews 9:26-28.*

"And He Himself is the propitiation for our sins, and not for ours only but **for the whole world,***" 1 John 2:2.* *"But this Man, after He had offered* **one sacrifice for sins forever,** *sat down at the right hand of God," Hebrews 10:12.*

"For such a High Priest was fitting for us, who is holy, harmless, **undefiled, separate from sinners**, *and has become higher than the heavens; who does not need daily, as those high priests, to offer up sacrifices, first for His own sins and then for the people's, for this* **He did once for all** *when He offered up Himself," Hebrews 7:26-27.*

"God was in Christ reconciling the world *to Himself,* **not imputing their trespasses to them,**" *2 Corinthians 5:19.*

By reconciling the world back to Himself, through the sacrifice of Jesus Christ, resulting in our justification, the Holy Spirit is now able to fill the spirit of those who, by faith, come to Jesus Christ. *"Much more then,* **having now been justified** *by His blood, we* **shall be saved** *from wrath through Him. For if* **when we were enemies** *we were* **reconciled to God** *through the death of His Son,* **much more**, *having been reconciled, we* **shall be** *saved by His life," Romans 5:9-10.* So how is it that the human-race has been reconciled back to God resulting in justification "to all men?"

The 'Law,' or the commandments of God are not subject to humanities opinions or beliefs. They are the requirements of God that must be obeyed if one is to be found righteous in the eyes of God – period! For only if you are perfectly righteous can you make it into the kingdom of God. You don't have to like the law, agree with it or even try to keep the law, however, without completely and fully fulfilling it, according to God's standard of perfection, the gate into eternal heavenly bliss (becoming a new creation through the born-again experience) will remain closed.

In God's eyes, a person must live a sinless life, by not violating or breaking even one of His commandments, intentionally or in ignorance. The good news (the gospel message) is that the requirements of the Law/commandments of God *have been fulfilled* for all humanity by the sinless and perfect life and death of Jesus Christ.

"After this, Jesus, knowing that ***all things were now accomplished,*** *that the Scripture might be fulfilled, said, "I thirst!" Now a vessel full of sour wine was sitting there; and they filled a sponge with sour wine, put it on hyssop, and put it to His mouth. So when Jesus had received the sour wine, He said**, "It is finished,"** and bowing His head, He gave up His spirit," John 19:28-30.* What was finished? What was accomplished? The days of keeping and following the law! *"For Christ is the* **end of the law** *for righteousness to everyone who believes," Romans 10:4.*

"The end of the law for righteousness" is telling us that keeping and following the commandments of God (the law), to become righteous by God's standard, has ended. Jesus took on the sins of the world – our sins (what a gift!), for every single person from the time of Adam to those who are alive at this moment up to the end of the age, even those who have not yet been born.

Jesus paying for the sins of the world through His perfect sacrifice means that He has removed the 'penalty of sin' from us by placing it upon Himself and *taking our punishment* that we may have the chance to spend eternity in heaven with God. There can only be a penalty if there exists a law, a rule or commandment that can be broken.

The commandments of God have continually been broken by every human being who has ever been put under His commandments. The penalty for breaking even one of God's commandments is death or separation from God for all eternity. The giving of the law started in the Garden of Eden with Adam and Eve by God giving only one commandment; *"And the Lord God commanded the man, saying "Of **every tree of the garden** you may **freely eat**; "but of **the tree** of the knowledge of good and evil, **you shall not eat**, for in the day that you eat of it you shall surely die," Genesis 2:16,17.*

God is now in the position of freely giving everyone who asks, eternal life, however, just because the world was reconciled and justified by the sacrifice of Christ on the cross, does not mean that the whole world was saved. *"Much more then, **having now been justified** by His blood, we **shall be saved** from wrath through Him. For if **when we were enemies** we were **reconciled to God** through the death of His Son, **much more**, having been reconciled, we **shall be** saved by His life," Romans 5:9-10.*

The phrase, "*much more, having been reconciled, we shall be saved*," stated above, means there is more and an even greater event that needs to take place after the removal of the penalty of sin and that is salvation! Even though 'reconciliation' and 'justification' have been accomplished for the whole world, salvation is contingent on a person accepting the free-gift of God's Holy Spirit by asking Jesus to be their Lord and Savior. *"If you knew the **gift** of God, and who it is who says to you, 'Give Me a drink,' you would have **asked Him** and He would have **given you** living water,"* John 4:10. The only thing Jesus asked of the Samaritan woman was for her to ask Him (the gift of God), for a drink of living water, for which He would have gladly given her, and to which He eventually did (read John 4:1-42).

What is also surprising in the story of the Samaritan woman in Chapter 4 of the Book of John is that Jesus agreed with the woman that she indeed spoke the truth of having a man who was not her husband. He, however, also added comments about her having five husbands, to which she replied; "Sir, I perceive You are a prophet." She knew Jesus had spoken correctly, yet she received no rebuke from Jesus, no scorn from Him or commandment to 'get right with God.'

*"For God so loved the world that He **gave His only begotten Son**, that whosoever **believes** in Him should **not perish** but have everlasting life,"* John 3:16.

*"For the bread of God is He who comes down from heaven and **gives life to the world**,"* John 6:33.

*"I am the light of the world. He who follows after Me shall not walk in darkness, but **have the light of life**,"* John 8:12.

*"Repent, and let every one of you be baptized in the name of Jesus Christ for the remission of sins; and you shall **receive the gift of the Holy Spirit**,"* Acts 2:38.

"God demonstrates His own love towards us, in that **while we were still sinners, Christ died for us**," Romans 5:8.

"But the **free gift** is not like the offense. For if by one man's offense many died, much more the grace of God and the **gift by the grace** of the one Man, Jesus Christ, abounded to many. And the **gift** is not like that which came through the one who sinned.

For the judgment which came from one offense resulted in condemnation, but **the free gift** which came from many offenses resulted in justification.

For if by the one man's offense death reigned through the one, much more those who receive abundance of grace and **the gift** of righteousness will reign in life through the One, Jesus Christ. Therefore, as through one man's offense Judgment came to all men, resulting in condemnation, even so through one Man's righteous act, **the free gift came to ALL MEN**, resulting in **justification**," Romans 5:15-18. "For the wages of sin is death, but **the gift** of God is eternal life in Christ Jesus our Lord," Romans 6:23.

CHAPTER 12

THE NEW CREATION

BORN OF THE SPIRIT

"Most assuredly, I say to you, unless one is born again, he cannot see the kingdom of God," John 3:3.

This is the last chapter of this book and by now you should have a pretty good idea of what it means to be born-again through the infilling of

God's Holy Spirit, as well as the understanding that only because of what Jesus Christ has done through his birth, death, resurrection and ascension back to God the Father, that becoming the *new creation* is possible. There is, however, more to becoming the 'new creation' (born-again) than just having God's Holy Spirit living in our spirit, there is much, much, more.

We now know that it is God's Holy Spirit that gives true *life* to our spirit and it is our spirit and soul that animates our body. Our soul/mind/consciousness is that part of who and what we are that allows us to take in the things of God, as well as the things of the world. Our spirit and soul animates our body whether we are saved or not. Biblically speaking, being alive and having life are two separate issues.

A person can be alive without having life (God's Holy Spirit living in their spirit). Having life, is having the kingdom of God living within your spirit, *"The kingdom of God cometh not with observation: neither shall they say, 'Lo, here! Or there! For lo, **the kingdom of God is within you**," Luke 17:21 (ASV),* or in other words, being born-again!

The concept of being, 'born again' is something that one should not get snagged on, mentally or conceptually. It's not that we won't get entangled on such an esoteric, mysterious and cryptic notion. It's just something that one should not 'marvel' at or even try to be intellectual or cerebral about the very words 'born-again' that Jesus used.

"There was a man of the Pharisees named Nicodemus, a ruler of the Jews. This man came to Jesus by night and said to Him, "Rabbi, we know that You are a teacher come from God; for no one can do these signs that You do unless God is with him." Jesus answered and said to him.

*"Most assuredly, I say to you, **unless one is <u>born again</u>, he cannot see the kingdom of God."** Nicodemus said to Him, "How can a man be born when he is old? **Can he enter a second time into his mother's womb and be <u>born again</u>?"** Jesus answered, "Most assuredly, I say to you, unless one is born of water and the Spirit, he cannot enter the kingdom of God. "That which is born of the flesh is flesh, and that which is born of the Spirit is spirit.*

*"**Do not marvel** that I said to you, "You must be born again," The wind blows where it wishes, and you hear the sound of it, but cannot tell where it comes from and where it is going, so is everyone who is <u>**born of the Spirit**</u>," John 3:1-8*

'Born-again' is the same thing as being 'born of the Spirit,' which is the same as having the 'kingdom of God within you.' When Jesus stated to Nicodemus, "do not marvel," He was telling him, as well as the future readers of the Bible, that he (Nicodemus, and we) should not be in awe of, amazed, or in wonder of the fact, that a person can be 'born *again.*'

Most people do not marvel over the fact that they exist, that they were born into this world without no prior approval as to whether they wanted to exist or not. Obviously, that is an impossibility because that would violate the foundations of logical thought; that no existing thing or person can cause itself or themselves to exist. That would mean they would have to exist and not exist, at the same time, to make themselves come into existence, a totally absurd proposition. This second birth that Jesus is talking to Nicodemus about, is diametrically opposed to the traditional way we come into this world. We come into this world with; no voice to say yes or no to our existence, no thought as to the gender we would like to exist as, no opinion as to the family or geographical location where we would like to live. We had no say so whatsoever concerning all the 'particulars' of our first birth. That, however, is not the case for the second birth. How is this so?

Jesus was affirming to Nicodemus, in John chapter 3, where Jesus was declaring to Nicodemus that he could, in fact, now; chose to be *born-again*. Nicodemus could now choose to exist or not exist in the kingdom of God, be or not be like the angels, be or not be a child in the family of God, be or not be part of His church, partake or not partake of His divine nature, live in or not live in eternal heavenly bliss with God Himself.

Jesus was telling Nicodemus that we now have a say-so as to whether we want to be born-*again*. This is the second birth and it is *our choice*. If we say yes to being born-again, then we become a child of the Most-High God, the creator of all creation. *"Behold what manner of love the Father has bestowed on us, that we should be called the children of God!" 1 John 3:1.*

Born-again believers get all the benefits of God's holy kingdom! Think about that for a moment. ALL the benefits of heaven while existing in an indestructible spirit, soul and a new *spiritual* body. This is what it means when the Bible declares that Jesus became like us that we may become like Him. *"In the beginning was the Word, and the Word was with God, and* **the Word was God." "And the Word became flesh and dwelt among us,"** *John 1:1,14. "by which have been given to us exceedingly great and precious promises, that through these* **you may be partakers of the** *divine nature*, *having escaped the corruption that is in the world through lust,"* 2 Peter 1:4. Jesus partook or our nature that we may partake of His nature. That, in part, is what being born-again means.

We must take on the nature of God Himself if we are to live with Him in His kingdom forever. Living in the kingdom of God for all eternity is granted only to His children and a person can only be a child of God if he is adopted into His family. 'Adoption into the family of God' is another way to say that a person is born-again. *"For you did not received the spirit of bondage again to fear, but you received the* **Spirit of Adoption** *by whom we cry out,* **"Abba Father."** *The Spirit Himself bears witness with our spirit that* **we are children of God."** *Roman 8:15,16.* This passage of scripture clearly indicates that we become His children when we are born-again. Jesus also distinctly indicated that becoming 'like a child' was a hallmark of a born-again person, *"Assuredly, I say to you, unless you are* **converted** *and* **become** **as little children***, you will by no means enter the kingdom of heaven,"* Matthew 18:3.

Being a 'child of God,' a 'child,' and 'as a child' are three distinctly different concepts. Every *born-again believer*, regardless of their age, is a 'child of God,' in the same way that every person; adult, adolescent or baby, is a child to their parents. If you are born-again, God is your Father, your heavenly Father. Being a 'child,' is being a non-adult, and is also dependent on a person's age and culture they live in, as well as the condition of their mental, emotional and intellectual well-being.

Being 'like a child' is when an adult takes on the certain mental, emotional and personality traits that a child possesses. So, what is it that a child possess that Jesus would like us to also possess or be like? Let's go back to the above-mentioned scripture, but this time in context to, as Paul Harvey would say, "the rest of the story."

The disciples, having been around Jesus for quite some time and having seen and partaken of the power of the Holy Spirit by engaging in the workings of miracles, are now thinking they are pretty hot stuff. They are now conjuring up in their own vain imaginations, who is the greatest among themselves. They, however, mask over their real intentions by asking Jesus, *"Who then is greatest in the kingdom of heaven?" Matthew 18:1,* Not 'who is the greatest among them,' but Jesus, already knowing their hearts and their thoughts, *"called a little child to Him, set him in the midst of them, and said, "Assuredly, I say to you, unless you are **converted** and **become as little children**, you will by no means enter the kingdom of heaven. "Therefore, whoever humbles himself as this little child is the greatest in the kingdom of heaven."* Matthew 18:2-4. He then adds, *"Whoever receives one little child like this in My name receives Me,"* Matthew 18:5.

Notice that the disciples, asking about someone already in the kingdom of heaven, are met with an answer about persons not in the kingdom of heaven, but rather here on earth, and what a person must do to enter the kingdom of heaven; be converted (born-again) and become *as* a little child. This answer spoke directly to their hidden thoughts. That is what is so masterful about our divine Lord when it comes to answering any question(s). He always goes to the heart of the matter because He knows the thoughts and intentions of every person, something only God can know.

Another very interesting thing about the above story is that it is totally opposite of what we humans do here on earth. We as parents, teachers, counselors, etc., take a child and surround them by figures of history, men and women of renowned status, point to them and try to encourage, motivate or influence that child, whether he or she be our own child, client or student, to become like famous and accomplished worldly heroes. We point our children to our worldly idols, but Jesus turned that idea upside down by pointing His disciples (who we consider 'great men of God' in the Bible), to a small child.

Jesus took a small child set him 'in the midst' of these 'great men of God' and did not tell the child to become like the disciples, but instead, He told the disciples to become like the child! Imagine the President of the United States visiting a small rural elementary school in somewhere in New Mexico and while he is standing in front of the classroom he is told that he needs to become like the children in that classroom, if he wants to really be someone of great importance!

Imagine the President of the United States being told that unless he is converted and becomes like a child, he cannot enter the kingdom of heaven. You must remember that unless you are or have been the President of the United States, it will be hard for you really grasp the reality of the intellectual, mental and emotional condition of someone of such great stature being told he must be converted and 'become as a child,' so he can to go to heaven, but nevertheless, that is what is required of that person, as per God's condition, to enter the kingdom of God for all eternity.

*"Then they brought little children to Him, that He might touch them; but **the disciples rebuked those who brought them**. But when Jesus saw it, **He was greatly displeased** and said to them, "Let the little children come to Me, and do not forbid them; for of **such is the kingdom of God**. "Assuredly, I say to you, whoever does not receive the kingdom of God **as a little child will by no means enter it.**" Mark 10:13-15.* If the Presidents, Queens and Kings of the world need to become as a child to enter the kingdom of God, what must the kingdom of God be like? The answer is 'born-again' *children* of God! *"having been **born again** not of corruptible seed but incorruptible, through the word of God which lives and abides forever," 1 Peter 1:23. "Behold what **manner of love** the Father has bestowed on us, that **we should be called the children of God!**" 1 John 3:1.*

"But children can be mean, hurtful, sneaky, devious, selfish, right?" As a Mental Health Therapist who has worked with children for over 20 years, the answer to that question is, "most certainly they can," but they are also very trusting, quick to believe and most important, they are *innocent* in the eyes of God, despite their sinful thoughts, words or deeds. You must become innocent in the eyes of God, just as children are innocent in the eyes of God.

The wonderful news is that you can become innocent in the eyes of God, but only if you accept the free-gift of God's Holy Spirit. However, first you must believe that Jesus is who He says He is, and has done what it is

He claims He has done for you. It can only happen to you once and only by *coming to Jesus*, believing that He died for your sins, repenting of your sins and trusting in the name of Jesus Christ, the Son of God, who then, through the infilling of the Holy Spirit, gives life to your 'dead-to-God' spirit causing your *spirit* to be 'born-again!'

This heavenly gift is not exclusive to the rich, the intellectual, the religious or any other type of exclusive group, but rather, it is inclusive of all humanity. God's will is that none would perish and that all should be saved, however, *"Enter by the narrow gate; for wide is the gate and broad is the way that leads to destruction, and there are many who go in by it. "Because **narrow** is the gate and **difficult** is the way which leads to life, and there are **few who find it,"** Matthew 7:13.* The gate is narrow because there is no salvation or eternal life in heaven with the Father except through His Son, Jesus the Christ. It is difficult because unless you 'become as a child,' your adult mentality, religious or non-religious experience, and intellect will most definitely get in the way of seeing and understanding your need to be 'born-again.'

God is not concerned with the condition you are in when you come to Him. His concern is whether you accept or reject Him. But whatever condition it is that you are in when you come to Him, He is not only willing, but also wanting to bless you with the gift of true life, starting here on earth and culminating in the heavenly realms with an inheritance beyond human imagination.

When you come to Jesus;

1. Dead: _He gives you eternal life_; _"For God so loved the world that He gave His only begotten Son, that whoever believes in Him should not perish, but **have everlasting life**," John 3:16. "Most assuredly, I say to you, he who hears My word and believes in Him who sent Me **has everlasting life**, and shall not come into judgment, but has **passed from death into life**," John 5:25_

2. Naked: _He clothes you with righteousness_; _"I will greatly rejoice in the Lord, My soul shall be joyful in my God; For He has clothed me with the garments of salvation, He has covered me with the **robe of righteousness**," Isaiah 61:10. "For we know that if our earthly house, this tent, is destroyed, we have a building from God, a house not made with hands, eternal in the heavens. For in this we groan, earnestly desiring to be **clothed with our habitation which is from heaven**, if indeed, **having been clothed**, we shall not be found naked. For we who are in this tent groan, being burdened, not because we want to be unclothed, but further clothed, that mortality may be swallowed up by life," 2 Corinthians 5:1._

3. Frightened/Fearful: _He gives you peace_; _"Be anxious for nothing, but in everything by prayer and supplication, with thanksgiving, let your requests be made known to God, and the **peace of God**, which surpasses all understanding, **will guard your hearts and minds** through Christ Jesus," Philippians 4:6,7. "For He Himself **is our peace**, who has made both one,_

and has broken down the middle wall of separation, having abolished in His flesh the enmity, that is the law of commandments contained in ordinances, so as to create in Himself one new man from the two, thus making peace and that He might reconcile them both to God in one body through the cross, thereby putting to death the enmity," Ephesians 1:4. "For God has not given us a spirit of fear, but of power and of love and of **a sound mind**." 2 Timothy 1:7.

4. Unsure/Insecure: _He gives you certainty of truth_; "If you abide in my word, you are my disciples indeed. And you shall know **the truth** and the truth shall make you free... therefore if the Son makes you free, you shall be free indeed," John 8:31,31, 36. "I am the Way, **the Truth**, and the Life. No one comes to the Father except through Me," John 14:6. "If you love Me, keep my commandments. And I will pray the Father, and He will give you another Helper that He may abide with you forever, **the Spirit of Truth**, whom the world cannot receive, because it neither sees Him nor knows Him, but **you know Him, for He dwells with you and will be in you**," John 14:15-17.

5. Poor: _He makes you rich_; "And My God shall supply **all your needs** according to His riches in glory by Christ Jesus," Philippians 4:19. "He who did not spare His Own Son, but delivered Him up for us all, how shall He not with Him also **freely give us all things**?" Romans 8:32.

6. Rich: *He makes you compassionate;* *"Now behold, there was a man named Zacchaeus who was a chief tax collector, and he was rich. And he sought to see who Jesus was, but could not because he was of short stature. So he ran ahead and climbed up into a sycamore tree to see Him, for He was going to pass that way. And when Jesus came to the place, He looked up and saw him, and said to him, "Zacchaeus, make haste and come down, for today I must stay at your house. So he made haste and came down, and received Him joyfully. But when they saw it, they all complained, saying, "He has gone to be a guest with a man who is a sinner." Then Zacchaeus stood and said to the Lord, "Look Lord, I give half of my goods to the poor; and if I have taken anything from anyone by false accusations, I restore four-fold,"* Luke 19:2-8.

7. Sorrowful: *He gives you joy;* *"Most assuredly, I say to you that you will weep and lament, but the world will rejoice; and you will be sorrowful, but your sorrow will be turned to joy,"* John 16:20. *"And I heard a loud voice from heaven saying; Behold, the tabernacle of God is with men, and He will dwell with them, and they shall be His people, God Himself will be with them and be their God. And God will wipe away every tear from their eyes; there shall be no more death, nor sorrow, nor crying. There shall be no more pain, for the former things have passed away,"* Revelations 21:3.

8. Ashamed: *He gives you confidence;* *"…according to the eternal purpose which He accomplished in Christ Jesus our Lord, in whom we have boldness and access with confidence through faith in Him,"* Ephesians

*3: 11,12. "And now little children, abide in Him that when He appears, **we** **may have confidence** and not be ashamed before Him at His coming," 1 John 2:28. "**Being confident** of this very thing, that He who has begun a good work in you will complete it until the day of Jesus Christ," Philippians 1:6.*

9. Lowly: <u>He lifts you up</u>; *"Humble yourself in the sight of the Lord and **He will lift you up**," James 4:10. "Save your people and bless your inheritance; Shepard them also, and **bear them up forever**," Psalms 28:9.*

10. Without faith: <u>He gives you faith</u>; *"For I say, through the grace given to me, to everyone who is among you, not to think of himself more highly than he ought to think, but to think soberly, as **God has dealt to each one a measure of faith**," Romans 12:3.*

11. A Stranger: <u>He befriends you</u>; *"Greater love has no one than to lay down ones' life for his friends. **You are my friends** if you do whatever I command you. No longer do I call servants, for a servant does not know what his master is doing; but **I have called you friends,** for all things that I heard from My Father I have made know to you," John 15:13-15.*

12. Seeking: <u>He gives you true knowledge and wisdom</u>; *"Settle it in your hearts not to meditate beforehand on what you will answer; for I will gives you a mouth and **wisdom** which all your adversaries will not be able to contradict or resist," Luke 21:14,15. "However, **we speak wisdom** among those who are mature, yet not the wisdom of this age, nor of the rulers of*

this age, who are coming to nothing. But **we speak the wisdom of God** *in a mystery, the hidden wisdom which God ordained before the ages for our glory," 1 Corinthians 2:6,7.*

13. Confused: *He gives you true meaning and enlightens you;* "*For you will light my lamp; The Lord will* **enlighten my darkness**," *Psalms 18:28. "That the God of our Lord Jesus Christ, the Father of glory, may* **give to you the spirit of wisdom and revelation in the knowledge of Him, the eyes of your understanding being enlightened; that you may know what is the hope of His calling,** *what are the riches of the glory of His inheritance in the saints, and what is the exceeding greatness of His power toward us who believe," Ephesians 1:17,17.*

14. Lost: *He gives you direction and purpose;* "*It was right that we should make merry and be glad, for your brother was dead and is alive again, and* **was lost and is found**," *Luke 15:32. "And we know that all things work together for good to those who love God,* **to those who are called according to His purpose,** *for whom He foreknew, He also predestined to be conformed to the image of His son, that He might be the firstborn among many brethren. Moreover,* **whom He predestined, these He also called; whom He called, these He also justified, and whom he justified, these He also glorified,**" *Romans 8:28-30.*

15. Abandoned/Homeless: *He gives you a kingdom;* "*Can a woman forget her nursing child, and not have compassion on the son of her womb?*

*Surely they may forget, yet **I will not forget you, see, I have inscribed you on the palms of My hands**,"* Isaiah 49:15. *"Let not your heart be troubled; you believe in God, believe also in Me. **In my Father's house are many mansions**; if it were not so, I would have told you. And if I go and prepare **a place for you, I will come again and receive you to Myself; that where I am, there you may be also**,"* John 14:1-4. *"If anyone loves Me, he will keep My word; and My Father will love him, and **We will come to him and make Our home with him**,"* John 14:23. *"And do not seek what you should eat or what you should drink, **nor have an anxious mind**. For all these things the nations of the world seek after, and your Father knows that you need these things, But, seek the kingdom of God and all these things shall be added to you. Do not fear, little flock, for **it is your Father's good pleasure to give you the kingdom**,"* Luke 12:29-33.

JOHN 3:16

Made in the USA
Las Vegas, NV
15 January 2022

41531994R00116